School of Visual Arts
Masters in Branding

A History of Brands

Origins of Consumer Markets

Richard Shear

Series Foreword by Debbie Millman

ROCKPORT

Quarto.com

© 2025 Quarto Publishing Group USA Inc.
Text © 2025 Richard Shear

First published in 2025 by Rockport Publishers, an imprint of The Quarto Group,
100 Cummings Center, Suite 265-D, Beverly, MA 01915, USA.
T (978) 282-9590 F (978) 283-2742

Rockport Publishers titles are also available at discount for retail, wholesale, promotional,
and bulk purchase. For details, contact the Special Sales Manager by email at specialsales@
quarto.com or by mail at The Quarto Group, Attn: Special Sales Manager, 100 Cummings
Center, Suite 265-D, Beverly, MA 01915, USA.

10 9 8 7 6 5 4 3 2 1

ISBN: 978-0-7603-9517-2

Digital edition published in 2025
eISBN: 978-0-7603-9518-9

Library of Congress Cataloging-in-Publication Data available

Design: Mark Kingsley
Page Layout: Megan Jones Design
Photography: Alamy: pages 17, 19 (both), 21, 22, 25, 29, 31 (both), 32, 33 (both), 35 (all), 37, 39, 41,
    43 (both), 45, 47, 48, 49, 52, 55 (all), 56, 60, 61 (both), 65 (both), 67 (all), 70, 71 (all), 73, 74 (both),
    75 (right), 79 (all), 81 (bottom left, top right), 87 (left), 88, 89, 91, 92, 93, 95 (both), 98, 99, 100,
    103, 104, 105, 106, 111 (top right), 112, 113, 116, 117, 119 (both), 120 (right), 123, 124, 126 (both), 128,
    131 (top left and top right), 132 (right), 135 (both), 136, 137, and 140; Jones Knowles Ritchie:
    page 4; Shutterstock: page 85 (top); Paula Scher/Pentagram: page 75 (left); Invok Brands:
    pages 142, 143, and 144; Quinton Meyer: page 154; Seth Mroczka: page 155
Series edited by: Mark Kingsley

Printed in Malaysia

For my wife, Pam, who has been a lifelong inspiration and has blessed me, every moment, with her sensitivity, encouragement, creativity, and love; and for our amazing children, Alex and Scott, who constantly inspire and remind me every day of the miracles life provides.

This series of books is an offering from the School of Visual Arts Masters in Branding Program, the first and longest-running program of its kind in the world. This pioneering course of study provides a select group of graduate students an opportunity to study with some of the most accomplished brand experts working today.

Our intensive one-year graduate degree program is a challenging multi-disciplinary experience of lectures, real-world client projects, and unique and progressive workshops and includes the examination of classic business school case studies, individual one-on-one professional mentorship, and group and personal projects.

The foundation of the Master of Professional Studies in Branding is the deep exploration and understanding of the role brand strategy plays in business, behavior, marketing, and culture. The curriculum allows students to create frameworks to guide brand, design, and business development; critically evaluate brand, business, marketing, and design approaches; and master the intellectual link between strategy and creativity. In addition, we analyze marketing challenges involved in creating, sustaining, and reinventing brands that have fallen out of pace with culture. In a sentence, we work hard.

This remarkable series of books gathers together and documents the brand research and pedagogy we've been investigating and creating over the past fifteen years. The very faculty that have invented and developed this curriculum have codified their learning and their teaching for the first time in this manner.

We are proud to share this work with the world and with you.

Debbie Millman
Chair, Masters in Branding
School of Visual Arts

Contents

Introduction

I begin this book with an exercise asked of all students at the beginning of my brand history course in the Masters in Branding program at the School of Visual Arts. The exercise is to visualize and then describe your favorite brand.

Define the characteristics and experiences you appreciate about your brand, and then think of the aesthetic and cultural influences and historical precedents that influence your affinity for it, how it differentiates itself, and finally, the role its "brand community" plays in your life. It's sure to be a complex exercise, one whose purpose is to demonstrate that all brands must be viewed through the lens of time and lived experience.

Even if it is a new brand, it is likely that important historical events, perhaps centuries old, have meaningfully shaped its identity. It is precisely this understanding of brand context and its relevance in today's complex culture, and the lessons learned by connecting the past with today, that this book hopes to illuminate.

In a very personal way, I was recently reminded of how rich and varied those connections can be in a vivid moment that reflects the historical complexities described throughout this book. The story includes my father, an architect during the last half of the twentieth century, who early in life taught me two lessons: the importance of creativity and realization that the practice of design can actually be a viable life choice.

My sense of connection began at a screening of Jason Cohn's movie *Modernism Inc.*, a documentary on the life of twentieth-century architect Eliot Noyes. Grace Farms in New Canaan, Connecticut, where the film was shown, said in its introduction to the evening, "Noyes brought a not-before-seen modernist design approach to corporate America. His impact on companies like IBM and Mobil paved the way for Apple and many design-conscious brands we know today."

It suddenly struck me that I was connected, through a combination of genealogy and my life's work, to generations of designers who each made invaluable and unique contributions to the building of aesthetically and culturally significant brands:

- Peter Behrens was hired by the German industrial company AEG in 1907 as its first "Artistic Advisor" and went on to create one of the first comprehensive corporate design cultures.

- Walter Gropius passed through Behrens's AEG design group before leading the Bauhaus and was on the faculty at the Harvard Graduate School of Design from 1937 to 1952.

- Eliot Noyes graduated from the Harvard design program in 1938 after studying under Gropius and Bauhaus architect and furniture designer Marcel Breuer, going on to work in their Cambridge design firm. After serving in World War II, he started his own firm in New Canaan, Connecticut.

- My father, George Shear, worked for Noyes in the 1960s during one of the firm's most influential and iconic periods.

Every one of these individuals had a deep influence on my life's path. My inheritance of, and connection to, design through this genealogy is typical of the complex and at times unexpected way we view the historical events of the world and their diverse forms and is fundamental to how we respond to a brand. You, too, have shared connections to individuals and brands of the past that you are likely to discover throughout this book.

Since my class began in 2010, it continues to reveal the connections between past and present in an attempt to shape the future while building awareness of the rich legacy and growth of global consumer culture.

The path connecting the creation and historical evolution of brands and consumer markets is not a straight line. In the drawing of that line—however jagged, interrupted, and circuitous—we cover design aesthetics, anthropology, culture, marketing, retailing, technology, and media.

We live in an era, much like that of the mid-1400s, where culture and technology are radically altering the content, availability, and usage of information, a period marking the boundary between old and new . . . traditional and revolutionary.

The fifteenth and twenty-first centuries are also both periods that reflect "the drive to use meaning to create profit" as Chandra Mukerji describes in her book *From Graven Images*. There are few simpler definitions of a brand than this.

This book will connect historical, cultural, demographic, technological, commercial, and aesthetic dots that might seem unrelated. This brief and fast-paced journey will cover significant time periods with broad observations on culture, brands, and notable design events and practitioners.

Please note that throughout this book, I often combine two words from the previous paragraph into the term "commercial aesthetic." I simply define a commercial aesthetic as a business ideology where imagination meets purpose.

Thus, in the context of this book on a history of brands, the term describes how all elements of a commercial enterprise can be marshaled to create a unique and memorable brand using the creative tools and aesthetics available at that moment in history.

Understanding what contributes to this term's meaning—how this meaning evolves through history and what cultural issues impact it—is necessary to understand the growth of brands through the centuries. Every section of this book will present examples of that evolution.

We begin in the mid-1400s with a discussion of how print media—much more than books—dramatically expanded access to a vast variety of cultural information.

We then spend the sixteenth and seventeenth centuries reviewing the birth of consumer markets driven by the egos and eccentricities of Elizabeth I and Louis XIV while also tracing the beginnings of large-scale global consumer markets with a look at Native American trade and the formation of the British East India Company.

Our path continues into the eighteenth century, where I will try to convince you, by exposing their shockingly similar business practices, that Steve Jobs was the reincarnation of the British potter Josiah Wedgwood.

The next step in our journey takes us to the nineteenth century, where we review three new radical innovations in retailing—the department store, chain store, and mail-order house—each supported by revolutions in industry, transportation, and communications as well as by cultural shifts like migration and urbanization.

Our nineteenth century journey ends during a period that many define as the golden age of the poster: an iconic media format that has been a critical tool for brand builders.

We enter the twentieth century describing brands and individuals who captured that era's spirit of radical change and built brands with emerging new media: Peter Behrens, Procter & Gamble, Kodak, Coco Chanel, C. Coles Phillips, Paul Rand, and Alex Steinweiss.

As we move through the twentieth century, we will discuss the evolving consumer movement, the Greatest Generation of brands, suburban growth in the 1950s, and the spirit of revolution in the 1960s.

In the last three sections, our path begins to connect the present and past, and we regard the current and future place for brands. We will trace the death and (re)birth of the supermarket—evolving across four periods of transformation. We will then learn the four universal forms of search, from our hunter-gatherer culture to Google. And finally, I will present recommendations for the future of an evolving retail marketplace through the lens of the seven virtues: temperance, wisdom, courage, justice, faith, hope, and love.

We are now entering the sixth century of a slow-motion consumer revolution, where cultural, economic, technological, religious, political, and scientific change is continual, occasionally dramatic. As the cultural anthropologist Grant McCracken notes in the very first page of *Culture and Consumption*, "the great transformation of the West included both an 'industrial revolution' but also a 'consumer revolution.' . . . The consumer revolution is now seen to have changed Western concepts of time, space, society, the individual, the family, and the state."

McCracken and I share the feeling that the two eras—the 1400s and today—are similar, and throughout this book we will explain the implications for brands of these following phenomena:

- Time seems to be speeding up.

- Space seems to be shrinking.

- Society is becoming more interdependent.

- The individual is becoming less private.

- The family is more diverse.

- The state is more democratic.

The Origins of Consumption

1

PATTERNS AND PRINTS—DISTRIBUTORS OF INFORMATION AND MEANING

All forms of print media, not just books, played a vital role in the mid-1400s as educator, entertainer, record keeper, and cultural influencer. We could say that print was the "social media" of its time—and I use that term fully knowing its implications. This is the first of my "modern analogies" presented throughout this book, comparing an element from the past with a modern equivalent.

Let's begin with Grant McCracken, who makes this contention in *Culture and Consumption*: "The consumer revolution . . . may have been the first time . . . a human community willingly harbored a non-religious agent of social change."

In the 1440s, Johannes Gutenberg's moveable type revolutionized book publishing and in so doing allowed media access to individuals who were neither clergy, royalty, nor wealthy.

Within just four decades, Gutenberg's innovation had become universal. Historian Marcantonio Sabellico was given the first "Printing

Privilege," or copyright, in 1486 for his work *Decades rerum Venetarum*, a history of Venice. The Venetian legislature said,

> *The history of our city, written by the very learned Marcus Antonius Sabellicus from Rome, deserves for its eloquence and historical veracity to come into full public view. Therefore we, the undersigned noble Councilors, have debated and decreed that the aforementioned work by the aforenamed Marcus Antonius can be entrusted to some expert printer to print, at his own expense, and to publish the said work in such a manner as befits a polished history worthy of immortality; furthermore, we shall not permit anyone other than him to have the said work printed, under penalty of the displeasure of the most serene Signoria and a fine of 500 ducats.*

This simple paragraph lists five important elements as part of the copyright.

- The city's history needed to be written.

- It should be printed to ensure "immortality."

- Sabellico would write and print the history.

- They didn't want to pay for his efforts.

- In exchange, they gave him exclusive copyright.

In 2010, 524 years after it was first published, Google scanned and digitized *Decades rerum Venetarum*, making it available online for free. This supports the notion that print, as we have known it, is dead, and the nearly six-hundred-year reign of books—and other printed forms of communication—is clearly over.

Today's media environment is dominated not by ink and paper but by the hardware and software applications of digital technologists. Similarly, Johannes Gutenberg and Albrecht Dürer also witnessed a media revolution. Gutenberg created the "hardware" for the printing revolution, and as a printmaker, Dürer's talent was using this new print platform in ways that influenced both creativity and culture.

We are redefining, as did Gutenberg and Dürer, the responsibilities of the writer, artist, publisher, patron, distributor, and consumer. Using a modern analogy, Gutenberg created the printing hardware that brought book publishing into a new era. Dürer and other artists were

Opposite: The Gutenberg Bible

Incipit epla sci Jeronimi ad Paulinum presbiteru de omnibus diuine hystorie libris · Capitulum Primum ·

Rater ambrosius tua michi munuscula perferens · detulit simul z suauissimas litteras: que a principio amiciciaz fide probate iam fidei et veteris amicicie pferebant. Vera eni illa necessitudo e et xpi glutino copulata: quia non vtilitas rei familiaris · non psentia tantu corpoz · non subdola z palpans adulato: sed dei timoz · et diuinaz scripturaz studia conciliant. Legimus in veteribz historijs quosda lustrasse puincias · nouos adijsse pplos · maria trasisse: ut eos quos ex libris nouerat: coram q viderent. Sic pitagoras memphiticos vates · sic plato egiptum z architam tarentinu · eamq oram ytalie · que quonda magna grecia dicebat: laboriosissime peragrauit: et ut qui athenis mgr erat · z potens: cuiusq doctrinas achademie gignasia psonabant: fieret peregrinus atq; discipulus: malens aliena verecunde discere: q sua impudenter ingerere. Deniq; cum litteras quasi toto orbe fugientes psequitur: captus a piratis et venundatus · tyranno crudelissimo paruit · ductus captiuus vinctus et seruus: tamen quia philosophus: maior emente se fuit · ad tytumliuiu · lacteo eloquentie fonte manantem · de ultimis hispanie galliaruq finibus quosdam venisse nobiles legimus: et quos ad contemplationem sui roma non traxerat: vnius hominis fama perduxit. Habuit illa etas inauditum omnibus seculis · celebranduq miraculum: ut urbem tantam

ingressi: aliud extra urbem quererent. Apollonius siue ille magus ut vulgus loquitur · siue phus ut pitagorici tradunt · irrauit psas · ptrasuit caucalu · albanos · scithas · massagetas · opulentissima indie regna penetrauit: et ad extremum latissimo physon amne trasmisso puenit ad bragmanas: ut hyarcam in throno sedente aureo · z de tantali fonte potantem · inter paucos discipulos · de natura · de moribz ac de cursu dieru z sideru audiret docentem. Inde p elamitas · babilonios · chaldeos · medos · assyrios · parthos · syros · phenices · arabes · palestinos · reuersus ad alexandria · perrexit ad ethiopiam: ut gignosophistas z famosissimam solis mensam videret i sabulo. Inuenit ille vir vbiq; quod disceret: z semp proficiens · semper se melior fieret. Scripsit super hoc plenissime octo voluminibus: phylostratus.

Quid loquar de seculi hominibz: cum apostolus paulus · vas electionis · et magister gentium · qui de conscientia tanti in se hospitis loquebatur · dicens. An experimentum queritis eius qui in me loquitur cristus: post damascum arabiaq; lustratam ascenderit iherosolima ut videret petru et maseret apud eum diebus quindeci. Hoc enim misterio ebdomadis et ogdoadis: futur gentium predicator instruendus erat. Rursuq; post annos quatuordecim assumpto barnaba et tyto · exposuit cum apostolis euangelium: ne forte in vacuum curreret aut cucurrisset. Habet nescio quid latentis energie viue vocis actus: et in aures discipuli de auctoris ore transfusa: forti sonat. Unde et eschines cu rodi exularet · et legeret illa demostenis

the equivalent of software developers who used the platform to create new forms of print media.

Bill Gates and Paul Allen, the innovative architects of the personal computer operating system and digital word processing platform, are twentieth-century Gutenbergs. And in creating revolutionary new applications, developers like Mark Zuckerberg are the new Dürers.

But you are the Gutenbergs and Dürers of today.

One of the fundamental differences between then and now is that digital media allows us to be any one of those links in the information chain. And we are redefining the cultural impact of this new system of information distribution.

Cultural anthropologists Grant McCracken and Chandra Mukerji have described this period as pivotal to the creation of today's brand-driven consumer markets. In *Graven Images*, Mukerji mentions that the birth of printing with moveable type was "the first mass production technology which allowed for the creation of exactly identical objects."

A vital consideration for the development of contemporary brands is the ability to promise consistency. Consumer product companies must be able to produce and promise exactly identical objects.

She proposes that this period in Western Europe, and the associated materialistic accumulation of goods, was the first time a culture had enough disposable income that "the value placed on accumulation of goods for its own sake began to gain priority over other cultural values."

People were becoming more independent and less reliant on others. Literacy and books meant you could teach yourself. Yet printed media were not the only new objects contributing to people's independence and control. Clocks meant you didn't need to tell time from the sun, and maps meant you could know your location, navigate with less risk, and not ask for directions.

Trade in these objects was more than just an exchange of goods; it was an opportunity to communicate and exchange cultural knowledge. Artisans could manufacture for larger marketplaces, and their goods began to influence, and create, a more diverse world.

Opposite: Prints with various culturally significant images that both inform and entertain

New Products and New Markets

Producers were beginning to understand different markets and then developing designs for corresponding consumer groups. Mukerji describes this as "a system of meaning developed to make sense of the plethora of objects."

We associate the growth of printing only with the spreading of information. Yet its role in market development tends to be overlooked. The distribution of pictorial prints established a distinction between elite and mass culture, led to the development of objects for a mass audience, and increased consumption across diverse consumer and social sectors.

From the beginning of the sixteenth century, Europe experienced an explosive period in the production, trade, and consumption of new and novel consumer goods.

Qualitative changes in the aesthetics of these goods have been noted by historians. Less recognized are the changes in economic and consumer activity that they created. This influenced economic development, increased consumption, and eventually led to the development of what we now know as consumer brands.

These new modes of consumption transformed the social order, as consumers looked beyond the utility value of objects toward their market value. The uniqueness of an object's design and authorship introduced another aspect of value to a wider audience.

Pictorial prints contained new kinds of visual imagery, including patterns, botanicals, anatomies, engineering drawings, and maps. They were not only decorative but also informative.

By the middle of the sixteenth century, engravings and etchings became the favored medium due to their fidelity to detail. The Italian engraver Marcantonio Raimondi's system of cross-hatching was a common approach to rendering, which defined the standard look for images until the invention of photography. And Albrecht Dürer codified the proper methods of representation, which were previously commonly found in treatises on anatomy or perspective.

Dürer and Raimondi also used apprentices, which made print production more efficient. This led to mass production, which reduced costs, making prints more accessible to average consumers. The proliferation of prints shaped international patterns of taste because they were easy to transport and easy to understand, regardless of language.

The trading patterns of this period allowed the movement of artisans, artifacts, patrons, and raw materials, creating a pan-European culture. Illustrations of nature, architecture, drawing, and engineering supplemented and aided the understanding of written text.

Decorative prints were the first mass-market medium to standardize the image making of cultural ideas and the sciences. Illustrated books gave wider visibility to regional forms. Lace pattern books influenced the design of furniture, upholstery, interiors, and other decorations. Herbal prints and other botanicals were used as embroidery patterns. Gardening books influenced furniture makers' wood selections, and garden designers' tree choices. Maps clarified national and local boundaries, which simplified and stabilized exploration and trade.

The fifteenth and sixteenth centuries were a time when new kinds of printed goods flourished, expanding a general understanding of the world. And frequently these goods were conveyors of fashion, not just function.

Modern consumer brands were built upon the foundational lessons of this market.

Opposite: John Gerard, a prominent English herbalist, published the *Generall Historie of Plantes* in 1597. It would become one of the most popular gardening books of its time.

2

AN EARLY GLOBAL CONSUMPTION PATTERN

By 1000 CE, trade within the Americas was well-established, with informal and decentralized trade routes among native people within the Americas. For example, mother-of-pearl from the Gulf of Mexico has been found in Manitoba, and Lake Superior copper has been found in Louisiana.

The Cantino world map of 1502 was developed from the four voyages of Columbus, Pedro Álvares Cabral, Vasco da Gama, and the Corte-Real brothers, and shows European incursion into that established network.

Consumer markets in the deep forests of New York, Quebec, or Machu Picchu were as hierarchical as the Elizabethan royal court discussed in the next chapter. But unlike the increasingly centralized economies of Europe, economies of the Americas encompassed thousands of independent, loosely affiliated tribes.

Archeological excavations and trade records indicate the five products that were traded most heavily were cloth, tools, decorations, novelties, and food. It is worth noting the interdependencies and similarities of consumer markets on both sides of the Atlantic.

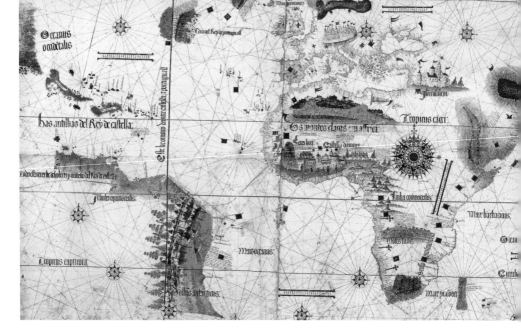

To illustrate this, consider the trade in European cloth, a very popular item for Native Americans. Animal skins, a decidedly old-tech staple, were traded for cloth, a newer technology. Woolen blanket material had obvious advantages. It was lighter than fur, dried faster, was more supple, remained warm when wet, could be fashioned with simple tools, and, unlike leather, did not need to be cured and dressed. Metal tools, another popular item, were brighter, more durable, and held an edge longer than traditional copper, bone, fired-clay, stone, or wood implements.

Trade with Europeans quickly became vital to the economies and people of North America. Excavations of sites in upstate New York dated from 1600 to 1620 indicate that only 10 to 15 percent of artifacts were of European origin. Barely two generations later, in sites dated from 1650 to 1655, fully 75 percent of material was of European origin.

In his book *1491*, Charles Mann points out the dark side of trade with Europeans. He describes the Americas of the time as "a thriving, stunningly diverse place, a tumult of languages, trade, and culture, a region where tens of millions of people loved, hated, and worshipped as people do everywhere."

As global trade became more widespread, whole villages throughout the region—now known as New England—simply disappeared from

Above: Cantino world map

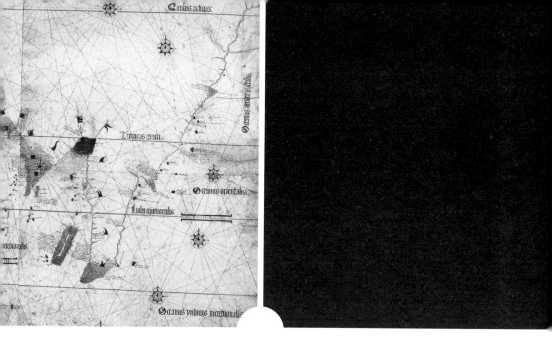

exposure to new diseases. This wasn't caused by one single event. It could have been brought by any of the more than two hundred vessels visiting from England by 1610 or by hundreds more from France, Spain, Portugal, and Italy.

In 1620, when the Pilgrims arrived in Massachusetts, they occupied a village that had been deserted by the Wampanoag tribe, who had been all but wiped out five years previously.

As Mann says, "So thorough was the erasure, that within a few generations, neither the conqueror nor the conquered knew that this world had existed."

This catastrophic population decrease through disease was also rampant across South America. Most scholars estimate that the total preconquest population of South America was 10 to 12 million, more than Europe. Yet the 1571 Spanish census estimated the postconquest number was just 1.5 million.

The Mayan city of Tiwanaku, and its surrounding area on the southern shores of Lake Titicaca, had a population of 365,000 in 1000 AD. Paris wouldn't exceed this until 500 years later. This would rank in the top 10 cities in the world at that time. And if we include the surrounding area, it would be in the top 5. In the early sixteenth century, only Beijing, Paris, Venice, and Constantinople would have been larger.

A quote from Bernal Díaz del Castillo, a conquistador traveling with Cortes, expresses the amazement shared by many Europeans when seeing Mexico City during this period:

*When we saw so many cities and villages built in the water and other
great towns on dry land we were amazed and said that it was like
the enchantments . . . on account of the great towers and cues and
buildings rising from the water, and all built of masonry. And some
of our soldiers even asked whether the things that we saw were not a
dream? I do not know how to describe it, seeing things as we did that
had never been heard of or seen before, not even dreamed about.*

The birth of a consumer society in the Americas was dependent on and,
many would say, caused by the growth of other global consumer cultures. And regardless of one's feelings on the topic, consumer society
comprised more than just European settlers.

Consumer growth was fully installed in the middle classes by the
early 1700s, supported by a significant increase in disposable income.
Consumption had clearly gone from necessity to fashion.

Animal pelts and skins were the currency of trade between the tribes of
the eastern woodlands and their colonial trading partners. Beaver was
in demand for broad-brimmed felt hats worn by European gentlemen.
Rare and luxurious furs from small animals like martin, otter, and fox
were used as trimming on extravagant women's gowns.

Dutch trading posts in Fort Orange (now Albany, New York) traded
forty-six thousand beaver pelts annually by the late 1650s. In 1614, the
French in Canada exported twenty-five thousand beaver skins back
to France.

Even twenty years after tribal populations had been cut in half by disease and warfare, Native American tribes still brought in thirty thousand pelts annually.

In the American South, the number of deerskins traded in the first
half of the 1700s was staggering. Two thousand Cherokee hunters in
the Carolinas harvested, on average, 12 deer a year, thus reducing the
herd's population by 1.25 million.

According to Mann, "trade between Native Americans and Europeans
in the 16th and 17th centuries fostered the first consumer revolution of
the Americas. This trade would also transform global society, creating
another kind of new world order—an environmental one."

Opposite: Roanoke American Indian town of Pomeiooc,
North Carolina, published by Theodor de Bry in 1588

As Mann and other historians and anthropologists have pointed out, babies born on January 2, 1494—the day Columbus founded La Isabela in the Dominican Republic—came into a world where direct trade and communication between Europe, the Americas, and East Asia was rare. By the time those babies had grandchildren,

- tobacco from the Caribbean was available to the wealthy and powerful in Madrid, Madras, Mecca, and Manila;

- group smoke-ins by violent young men in Tokyo would lead to the formation of two rival gangs;

- enslaved Africans mined silver in the Americas for sale to China;

- Spanish merchants waited for the latest shipments of Asian silk and porcelain from Mexico; and

- Dutch sailors traded cowry shells from the Maldives for human beings in Angola.

In *1493*, Mann discusses the beginning of what has become known as the Columbian Exchange: "[The] voyages of Columbus did not mark the discovery of a new world, but its creation. What happened after Columbus, was nothing less than the forming of a single new world from the collision of two old worlds."

By the nineteenth century, international trade had united the globe into a single ecological system. The Columbian Exchange, as Alfred W. Crosby called it in *Ecological Imperialism*, is the reason we have tomatoes in Italy, oranges in the United States, chocolates in Switzerland, and chili peppers in Thailand.

Mann continues,

> *To ecologists and environmental scientists, the Columbian Exchange is arguably the most important event since the death of the dinosaurs. It is true our times are different from the past. Our ancestors didn't have cell phones and the internet. But reading accounts of the creation of the world market one cannot help hearing echoes—some muted, some thunderously loud—of the disputes now on the television news. Events four centuries ago set a template for events we are living through today.*

3

ELIZABETH I AND THE ORIGINS OF CONSUMER MARKETS

All good brand identity stories begin with an epic adventure, and you know the highlights of this one.

In 1533, in the midst of English social evolution, a young princess was born to King Henry VIII and Anne Boleyn. Her parents divorced, she was declared illegitimate, and her mother was beheaded in 1536; this all happened as Henry broke away from the Catholic Church.

We can describe the evolution of her powerful brand by focusing on two issues. The first is the increasing role that personal consumption, specifically the kind that Elizabeth I encouraged for members of her royal court, had in transforming culture. The second is the "civilizing" process that resulted from this consumption.

Only recently have scholars begun to look at consumption's role in transforming culture, and certainly Elizabeth I played a distinct role in that cultural evolution.

As McCracken points out in *Culture and Consumption*, most history lessons only deal with legal, economic, industrial, or scientific issues, but there were other developments during this period. He points out a number of important changes, including new categories of goods; new times, places, and patterns of purchase; new marketing techniques; and new ideas about possessions and materialism. These changes led to new lifestyles, class mobility, product symbolism, and patterns of decision making.

The "Civilizing" Process

By the middle of the sixteenth century, Europe had undergone a "civilizing" process, creating complex standards of consumption, with table manners being one of the more obvious examples.

In 1533, Catherine de' Medici of Italy brought forks to her marriage with Henry II of France. According to a 1560 French manners book, different customs had developed in different European countries: Italians were known for using forks, Germans ate soup with spoons, and both German and Italian tables had a knife.

The Renaissance was thriving. Leonardo da Vinci, who had drawn the Vitruvian Man in 1487 and painted *Mona Lisa* in 1505, had been dead for almost thirty years. Michelangelo had completed the Sistine Chapel ceiling and *David* nearly forty years before. And Europeans were just beginning to use modern tableware.

On January 15, 1559, a twenty-six-year-old Elizabeth I was coronated in London. And from that day until her death in 1603, she lived a life filled with intrigue and complexity, fueled by an insatiable ego.

The most direct way to convey this epic saga—chronicling the development of a modern personal brand that dramatically altered the lifestyles of British royalty—is through portraits painted during Elizabeth's reign. They trace the evolution of her life and show how it became increasingly filled with symbolism, analogy, and meaning. Each portrait's artist clearly understood the critical importance of these visual clues. They became increasingly symbolic, with each work suggesting a story of a life filled with richness and complexity.

In 1560, Elizabeth I had been queen for a year. At twenty-seven, she is dressed quite plainly. This is one of the last portraits to focus on just her image rather than building an allegory of her life and surroundings.

At this time, London was a city in the early stages of an explosive growth that would see its population quadruple—from 50,000 in 1530 to 225,000 in 1605—and quadruple again to nearly 1 million by 1800. This was fueled by the growth of trade and commerce and the movement of European populations to urban centers.

To put this in perspective, in 1530 with a population of 50,000, London didn't rank among the world's top cities. Beijing was first in the world with 700,000 people. Cairo, ranked third, was the largest city in the Middle East with 400,000. And Paris was the largest in Europe with 185,000.

In 1575, having been on the throne for sixteen years, Elizabeth was consolidating her power and using expenditure as an instrument of governmental rule. As McCracken says, "Objects in the highly ceremonial context of the court began to formally communicate the legitimacy of her rule, aspirations for the Kingdom, qualities of power, and finally the godlike status as an individual in mythical, religious, and literary terms." The members of her court drove "a spectacular consumer boom as they began to spend with a new enthusiasm and on a new scale. In the process they dramatically transformed their world of goods and the nature of Western consumption."

Elizabeth is now forty-two years old. She is portrayed in the Pelican, Phoenix, and Darnley portraits with a "face of youth" technique used on all subsequent portraits. While each contains a simple pose, the majority of the canvas minimizes her face while maximizing the extremely complex and extravagant fashion, clearly meant to reflect a ruler obsessed with a formalized image and grandeur.

The Pelican portrait features imperial crowns over each of her shoulders—one above a rose and one above a fleur-de-lis. These images represent her claims to both England and France. The Pelican pendant on her breast symbolizes charity and redemption, and the queen's selfless love of her subjects.

Grant McCracken cites several observations of Elizabeth I during this time. She insisted that nobility foot the bill "for her expenditures on housing, hospitality, and clothing," forcing the court and her suitors to spend conspicuously on her behalf. Elizabeth then went on to encourage competitive spending in ways never previously seen. McCracken also notes that French historian Fernand Braudel suggested that the object was to make the court "a sort of parade, a theatrical spectacle . . . [and, with luxury] a means of government." For members of the court, it was not discretionary. If you wanted to be part of the court, you had to take part in these consumptive expectations.

This social competition expanded beyond the court into a general consumerism. McCracken describes these practices as seriously eroding "the cult of family status." Inherent in this idea was the notion that everything a generation did was a result of the efforts of the previous one, and that value must be considered for the next.

But the new competitive pressures of the Elizabethan court caused nobility to spend more for themselves and less on long-term benefits to their families.

Opposite: The Coronation portrait

An object's patina, the well-used appearance that older objects acquire with age, was becoming passé. Objects were increasingly looked at for their short-term benefit. Value came not from their patina but from their fashion and novelty.

In the 1580 Peace portrait, Elizabeth has been on the throne for twenty-one years and is in the midst of a turbulent conflict with Spain and the Netherlands. The portrait presents her as the messenger of peace with the olive branch in her right hand and a sheathed sword at her feet visually supporting this theme.

In the 1583 Sieve portrait, Elizabeth has been on the throne for twenty-four years. The sieve in her hand symbolizes chastity and purity, an idea from Petrarch's *Triumph of Chastity*.

Pictured in Nicholas Hilliard's 1585 painting known as the Ermine portrait, Elizabeth had ruled for twenty-six years. An ermine was the symbol of royalty, underscored by the gold crown. The crown also symbolizes majesty, while the queen's favorite colors—black and white—dominate the portrait's color palette in the background and her gown. Elizabeth also wears the famous "Three Brothers" jewel, one of her most cherished jewels, made of three rubies surrounding a triangular diamond. Two other highly symbolic objects are featured—the sword of state representing justice and an olive branch representing peace.

Filled with rich and complex symbolism, the 1588 portrait celebrated the defeat of the Spanish Armada. Three elements are worth noting. As symbols of purity, pearls are used to decorate her hair and gown. An imperial crown is positioned next to her right arm symbolizing her rule, and her hand is resting on a globe with her fingers over the western hemisphere.

Additionally, the victory over the Spanish armada is shown above her right shoulder.

In 1592, Elizabeth had been queen for thirty-three years. Sir Henry Lee, who commissioned this Ditchley portrait, used lavish entertainment as a means to regain her respect. The portrait commemorated Elizabeth's visit to his home in Ditchley and shows the queen standing above a map of England, and one foot resting near Ditchley.

Opposite left: The 1573 Pelican portrait

Opposite right: The 1583 Sieve portrait

Pictured in another Nicholas Hilliard portrait in 1599, Elizabeth is sixty-six years old and had been queen for over forty years. It was commissioned by the legendary Bess of Hardwick, who also embroidered the amazing sea serpents and dragons on the queen's skirt.

The Rainbow portrait, painted by Isaac Oliver around 1600, just three years before her death at the age of sixty-nine, is the most symbolic of them all. It now hangs at Hardwick Hall, and its website describes the portrait's complexity:

> *This portrait presents Elizabeth I in an iconic format. The Queen appears to float weightlessly over the rich carpet, the painter's attention firmly on the lustrous detail of the material surfaces. As in many other portraits of her, Elizabeth's costume—including her headdress, gloves and shoes—is encrusted with pearls. Even late into her reign these symbols of purity and virginity remained a potent aspect of her public persona.*

The Rainbow portrait again follows the pattern of increasing symbolism used in her portraits. Most significantly, it was painted when she was in her late sixties, yet it portrays the ageless nature of her mortality by illustrating her as young and beautiful.

Pearls are shown as a symbol of her virginity. Cynthia, goddess of the moon, is represented by a crescent shaped jewel.

A serpent symbolizing wisdom and a heart-shaped ruby held in the serpent's mouth, symbolizing the queen's heart, are intricately

embroidered on her left sleeve. This suggests that the queen's passions are controlled by her wisdom.

The words "No rainbow without the sun" are inscribed on the rainbow she holds in her right hand, suggesting that the queen's wisdom is the only thing that can guarantee peace and prosperity.

As a group, these portraits captured the life of a monarch concerned with the projection of power through complex visual symbolism and expressed the idea of status through symbolic objects.

This new focus on the ceremonial and symbolic precipitated a shift in the value of goods from patina to fashion. Elizabeth used conspicuous consumption to create a vast theater devoted to her support and power, setting in motion consumer behavior to come in the next century.

As a group, these portraits capture the life of a monarch who understood her role as the ultimate symbol of her country. McCracken suggests that in the highly ceremonial context of the court, these portraits began to "communicate the legitimacy of her rule, aspirations for the Kingdom, qualities of power, and the godlike status as an individual in mythical, religious, and literary terms."

Above: The 1588 Armada portrait

Opposite left: The 1599 Hardwick portrait

Opposite right: The 1600 Rainbow portrait

BRITISH EAST INDIA COMPANY—ONE OF THE FIRST GLOBAL CONSUMER BRANDS

Founded in 1600, the British East India Company was a unique enterprise in its scope, complexity, and domination of global trade. And it was one of Elizabeth I's most lasting contributions to the creation of global consumer markets—her royal charter for the founding of the Company in 1600 came just three years before her death.

The British East India Company—along with the Dutch East India Company, founded in 1602—ushered in an age of state-sponsored global trade. Elizabeth's charter gave the company a fifteen-year monopoly for English trade with India and the Far East. This put the organization in a position to become among the only multinational joint-stock corporations with the ability to wage war, negotiate treaties, coin money, and establish colonies.

It is interesting to note that the East India Company still exists in London and is owned by an entrepreneurial group from Mumbai. While the Company clearly had a checkered human rights record, the current company's website recognizes the complex nature of its history and influence: "Without the company our world would not be as it is today. It changed the world's tastes, its thinking, and its people, created new communities, trading places, cities, and shaped countries and commercial routes."

Singapore and Hong Kong were established by the company, and India was shaped and influenced by it. At one point the company controlled 50 percent of global trade and had the largest merchant navy in the world. The British and Dutch entities combined sent nearly 2 million Europeans to trade overseas on seven thousand ships.

The British East India Company orchestrated a number of symbols into one of the first global brand systems across three key divisions.

The Corporate Identity

The name of the Company's Coat of Arms, or official seal, was the Armorial Bearings of the Company of Merchants of London Trading into the East Indies. In it, sea lions and waving St. George pennants support a shield with three ships and roses. Open sails signify that the ships have a favorable wind. England is represented by roses, and the gold globe on top signifies the world.

At the top and bottom are the company's motto, "Deus Indicat. Deo Ducente Nil Nocet." meaning "God is our leader. When God leads, nothing can harm."

This Coat of Arms was granted by the King of Arms in 1600, with instructions from Elizabeth I. It was provided so the company would be recognized as having her royal patronage.

The Brand Identity

Initially a simple mark, it is still in use by the current company on various retail products. By the 1700s, the identity evolved into a heart-shaped figure surmounted by the mystical figure of four, or a sail. The merchant's mark was also referred to within the company as the "chop," a word derived from the Hindi word *ćhāp*, meaning "stamp."

Opposite top: British East India Company Leadenhall Street headquarters, a simple building completed in 1729

Opposite bottom left: The British East India Company Coat of Arms as designed in 1600

Opposite right: The merchant's mark, or "chop," stamped into a coin and used as a brand identity on packaging

Opposite bottom right: The East India Company flag, as adopted in 1801

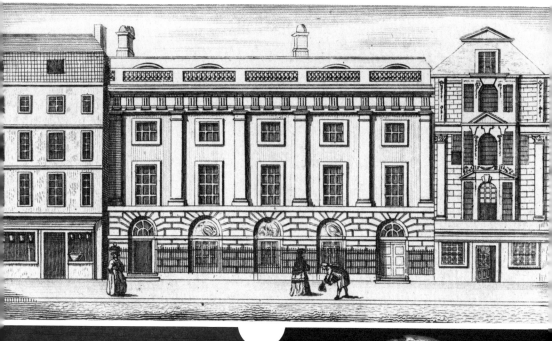

The merchant's mark not only showed that goods came from the East India Company, but it also signaled their quality. It was one of the earliest global commercial trademarks and became the most widely known brand logo of its time.

The Fleet Identity

The company fleet had a series of flags. The first was prior to the Acts of Union, and the second was used from 1707 to 1801, after the formation of the Kingdom of Great Britain. The last appeared in 1801, after the inclusion of Ireland, and flew until the middle of the nineteenth century.

Trade was so lucrative for such a long time that the Dutch East India Company was able to pay an astonishing 18 percent annual dividend for almost two hundred years. At that rate of return, one dollar invested in 1603 would be worth $3,299,904,702,716,151 USD in 1803—over 3 quadrillion dollars!

As mentioned, in a wonderful reversal of its heritage through the centuries, the company is owned today by a group from Mumbai that has a clear sense of the iconic brand, selling a variety of premium food products with a flagship store in the heart of London's Mayfair district.

We are a company, more than any other, born from the actions and endeavors of countless people over the centuries. It is the fusion of their lives, their cultures and their traditions which we respect in the choices we now make and in everything we now do. The Company continues its evolution and journey, but in all ways is still exploring, discovering, learning and connecting.

LOUIS XIV—THE BOURGEOISIE AND THE BAROQUE

"To be away from you, Sire, one is not only unhappy . . . one is ridiculous." —Anonymous French seventeenth-century individual

With the coronation of Louis XIV in 1643, consumption continued to be a political instrument and method of rule. This pattern, while certainly familiar to the approach taken by Elizabeth I a century earlier—to

---

Opposite: The Hall of Mirrors at Versailles

satisfy a ruler who was never satisfied—has two unique differences: the growth of the bourgeoisie and the Baroque.

Louis broke ground for Versailles in 1661. The Hall of Mirrors, with hundreds of mirrors that took craftsmen years to complete, could hold five thousand people and featured thirty-two silver chandeliers, handmade rugs, flowers, and orange trees in silver tubs. Furnishings, upholstery, and curtains changed seasonally, and the building was constantly being remodeled.

By the late seventeenth century, Versailles, just like the Elizabethan court, was the only place where nobles could receive royal attentions, including pensions, benefits, and positions in the church, army, and bureaucracy. This included a group of roughly five thousand people out of a French population of five hundred thousand—1 percent of the total.

Similar to Elizabeth's court, once admitted, one had to spend ruinously: gold and silver threads for clothing, stables of horses and kennels of dogs, carriages lined with velvet and painted panels, houses and furnishings fit for entertaining, and a support staff of servants, valets, and stable hands.

Like in England, the royals were almost universally in debt. Saddled with enormous expenses but without the King's ability to tax, they were forced to rely on the King for favors.

The Growth of the Bourgeoisie

Rosalind Williams wrote in her book *Dream Worlds*, "While nobles quarreled about precedence in the little 'country' of Versailles, in the great country outside, another hierarchy of social and economic standing had been forming."

Medieval divisions (royalty, clergy, and everyone else) were disappearing. The relatively open and prosperous Europe of the late seventeenth and early eighteenth centuries provided more employment options and opportunities to accumulate wealth, which led to a new consumer society.

The Baroque

Under Louis XIV, France became the most powerful country in Europe, militarily and culturally. Versailles and other large projects made profound contributions to the influence of French design.

By the late seventeenth century, Paris had replaced Rome as the Western world's arts capital. Louis's governmental policy instituted a new design infrastructure for funding and controlling the arts. This led to Cardinal Jules Mazarin's 1648 founding of the Académie des Beaux-Arts, where students were educated in drawing, painting, sculpture, engraving, and architecture.

Upon Mazarin's death in 1661, finance minister Jean-Baptiste Colbert assumed control over French artisanal production. The country would no longer purchase luxury goods from abroad but would itself set the standard for quality.

The Académie's domination over painting and sculpture was maintained through a hierarchy of genres, the "noblest" being historical painting with strong pictorial rhetoric and a strict sense of appropriate subject matter. An ideal example would be Poussin's *Holy Family on the Steps* from 1667.

In 1695, in another example of the interest in imposing an identifiable "French" style over all visual arts, Louis ordered a committee of scholars to develop a new typeface for the Imprimerie Royale, the royal printing office established in 1640 to improve the quality of French printing. It was charged to develop an alphabet with "new French letters that we have endeavored to render as agreeable as possible to the eye."

Opposite: Portrait of Louis XIV by Hyacinthe Rigaud, circa 1701

Additionally, since this typeface is standardized and grid based, it is another example of Louis's court establishing reliability and consistency, contributing to the perception of market stability.

Abbe Nicolas Jaugeon of the French Academy of Sciences was given the task. His Romain du Roi, cut by Philippe Grandjean, was reserved for the exclusive use of the Imprimerie Royale.

This cold but dignified typeface was first used in 1702. The new letterforms were designed to "scientific" principles. The calligraphic aspects of Gutenberg typography were no longer present. Based on a grid of 64 units, each was divided again into 36 smaller units for a total of 2,304 tiny squares.

The first publication to use this typeface was, appropriately enough, a history of the reign of Louis XIV, published in 1702.

Williams's closing comments connect the emergence of the bourgeoisie and the quality of the Baroque to the modern consumer society we find ourselves in today:

> Courtly life is dead . . . but the life of the consumer is more vigorous than ever, and therein lies the contemporary significance of the chateaux.

> These lords and ladies were the first people in modern society to experiment with discretionary consumption, to become familiar both with its intellectual and sensual pleasures and with its consequences of envy, vanity . . . seen from this perspective, the consumer revolution becomes far more than a rise in economic statistics or in available goods.

> Imitating their betters or challenging them . . . whether they were competing with their peers in a status war or merely putting social distance between themselves and their imitative lessers.

As McCracken says in *Culture and Consumption*, "It appears then that in the eighteenth century goods began to carry a new kind of status meaning. . . . The cultural meaning of goods was increasingly the way an anonymous society could maintain its center." Goods allowed Western societies to turn "into a miracle of existence . . . a cohesive society of perfect strangers."

Opposite: Examples of the Romain du Roi font

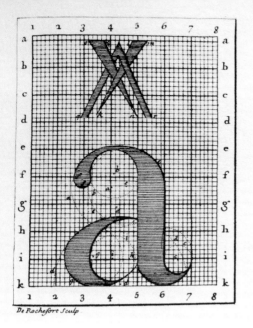
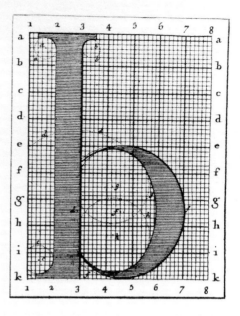

Within the span of just a few generations, objects that had once been the privileged possessions of the few were within reach of a much larger society. As English essayist Joseph Addison wrote in 1711,

> *Our Ships are laden with the harvest of every Climate: Our Tables are stored with Spices, and Oils, and Wines: Our Rooms are filled with Pyramids of China and adorned with the Workmanship of Japan. Our Morning's Draught comes to us from the remotest Corners of the Earth: We repair our Bodies by the Drugs of America and repose ourselves under Indian Canopies. My Friend Sir Andrew calls the Vineyards of France our Gardens; the Spice-Islands our Hot-beds; the Persians our Silk-Weavers, and the Chinese our Potters. Nature indeed furnishes us with the bare Necessaries of Life, but Traffic gives us greater Variety of what is Useful, and at the same time supplies us with everything that is Convenient and Ornamental.*

This expansion of consumer markets in Western society continued relentlessly for the next three hundred years.

6

JOSIAH WEDGWOOD—THE BEGINNINGS OF MODERN MERCHANDISING AND BRAND IDENTITY

In their book *The Experience Economy*, B. Joseph Pine II and James H. Gilmore observe that each successive wave of economic growth has been based on a distinct type of economic offering. For the early industrial era, it was the transition from commodities to goods to brands. Josiah Wedgwood was one of the earliest merchants to understand this transition and exploit it.

Wedgwood was born in 1730 in Staffordshire, England, as the eleventh child and youngest son of a mediocre potter. He was the fourth generation of potters in his family, which would continue for five more. As Neil McKendrick writes in *The Birth of a Consumer Society*, "The local Staffordshire ware was crude, the market still local, roads almost impassable, and the workmen unreliable."

But by the mid-1750s, the pottery market was improving. The records kept after the Weaver Navigation Act of 1721 show a six-fold increase in the traffic of pottery between 1739 and 1760. The growing demand for everyday earthenware was driven by tea consumption, along with expansion in the beer, coffee, and hot chocolate markets. Compared to earthenware, silver plate was more expensive, pewter was too scarce, and porcelain was too fragile.

To fully appreciate how Wedgwood capitalized upon this new economic period, it might be best to explore a side-by-side comparison with Apple's Steve Jobs. Wedgwood was one of the most "modern" merchants of his time, while Jobs was a "classic" technologist who built upon historical precedents—many tracing back to Wedgwood—in brand design, marketing, and customer experience.

Josiah Wedgwood lived in the early days of the industrial revolution, and Steve Jobs was present at the birth of another revolution: introducing the Apple Macintosh on January 22, 1984, in a now-iconic Super Bowl ad.

Opposite: Everyday earthenware in the mid-eighteenth century had a certain similarity—from England, Germany, and France. The contemporary parallel would be personal computers—like the IBM PC, Kaypro, and early Apple computers—looking very much alike.

The market for china in the 1750s was not much different from the personal computer market of the 1980s. Both made individual statements about one's place in an evolving culture. As Neil McKendrick comments, "It was Wedgwood's commercial triumph to turn that pursuit of ceramic luxury by the rich into the pursuit of useful (albeit fashionably desirable) pottery for the many. It required, in fact, one of the most brilliant and sustained campaigns in the history of consumer exploitation."

Both Wedgwood and Jobs dramatically changed the expectations of their industry, and the reasons that Josiah Wedgwood prospered are similar to Steve Jobs. Why is Apple a revolutionary brand? Like Wedgwood, the reasons include its design, usability, technology, sales, marketing, advertising, merchandising, logistics and distribution, retailing, and creative showmanship to create a compelling brand experience.

New Business Models

Wedgwood pioneered a new level of technical skill and division of labor. Like Apple, his early developments were quickly copied, and the form and function were reproduced. Some of Wedgwood's innovations include direct mail, money-back guarantees, traveling salesmen, self-service, free delivery, buy-one-get-one-free promotions, and illustrated catalogs.

Design

Both Wedgwood and Jobs saw the design process as integral to the brand's success:

> *"Beautiful forms and compositions are not made by chance, nor can they ever, in any material, be made at small expense. A composition for cheapness and not excellence of workmanship is the most frequent and certain cause of the rapid decay."* —Josiah Wedgwood

> *"In most people's vocabularies, design means veneer. It's interior decorating. It's the fabric of the curtains or the sofa. But to me, nothing could be further from the meaning of design. Design is the fundamental soul of a human-made creation that ends up expressing itself in successive outer layers."* —Steve Jobs

Quality

As McKendrick comments, "His selling policy relied on quality and above all fashionable appeal, and Wedgwood believed that high prices had an integral part to play in such policy."

> *"It has always been my aim to improve the quality of the articles of my manufacture, rather than lower their price."* —Josiah Wedgwood

> *"Be a yardstick of quality. Some people aren't used to an environment where excellence is expected."* —Steve Jobs

Innovation

Design and quality were not enough. Wedgwood had a long line of product and material innovations: green glaze, creamware, black basalt, jasper cameos, intaglios and seals, tea trays, snuffboxes, and Etruscan-styled painting.

Jobs introduced an operating system with a graphical user interface controlled by a mouse, continuing with the iPod, iPhone, iPad, iTunes, the Apple retail store, the App Store, and the Genius Bar.

Sales and Distribution

Wedgwood wanted to "achieve perfection in sales and distribution." Free shipping and the establishment of a London showroom supported his innovative spirit in this area.

Opposite: A label showing the London showroom return address and the "Carriage Paid" notation

Josiah Wedgwood & Byerley,

YORK-STREET, St. James's.

Carriage Paid.

LONDON.

Similarly, Jobs didn't just produce great hardware and elegant software. His innovations in sales and distribution practices have included iTunes, iOS apps, the Apple Store, Apple Cloud, and Apple TV.

Use of Influencers

Wedgwood was one of the first product marketers to "influence the influencers." He went after the monarchy, nobility, art connoisseurs, and fashion trendsetters of the time.

Royal patronage was a key tool used in his early marketing success. The names of his lines included Queens Ware, Royal Pattern, Russian Pattern, Bedford, Oxford, and Chetwynd. Each indicated his understanding that royal association would influence potential purchasers. In fact, he was the first to include these royal endorsements publicly on every billhead, order form, and advertisement.

A classic use of influencers was Catherine the Great's Frog Service, with 952 pieces for fifty place settings and 1,224 original paintings of well-known buildings and landscapes of England. Neil McKendrick, Lecturer in English Economic History at Cambridge University, vividly describes in an article in *The Economic History Review*, the frenzy in London when the service was put on public display, ticketed admission only, in a new showroom built expressly for the purpose. Day after day for over a month the "fashionable world thronged the rooms and blocked the street with their carriages."

The nobility and gentry anxiously assembling to view their homes and estates pictured on the service is absolutely analogous to the excitement that Apple generates with people lining up for the latest Apple releases.

British Ambassadors as Global Salesmen

By the 1770s, Wedgwood was looking for outlets that could offer new exposure to lines that had outlived their popularity in England. He cultivated the diplomats of the time by offering them free samples of his work that they were encouraged to bring with them on their respective worldwide travels.

Brand Positioning

Using the influence of powerful and important people was only one of the techniques employed by Wedgwood. He also used a number of other innovative techniques including warehouses, showrooms, exhibitions, trademarks, new standards of display, and articles in the press.

> "We agreed that those customers who were more fond of show and glitter, than fine forms . . . would buy Soho [a competing pottery brand], and that all those who would feel the effects of fine outline or had the veneration for antiquity would be with us." —Josiah Wedgwood

> "Pretty much, Apple and Dell are the only ones in this industry making money. They make it by being Wal-Mart. We make it by innovation." —Steve Jobs

Commemorative Ware

Being a member of the Society of Friends, informally known as the Quakers, and thus a fervent abolitionist, Wedgwood produced a famous jasper medallion with a kneeling slave, surrounded by the text "Am I not a man and a brother." He sent a consignment to his friend Benjamin Franklin in Philadelphia, where the pieces became a fashion statement for abolitionists and antislavery sympathizers and soon extended to the general public. This medallion is an early example of corporate social responsibility, which is a standard branding practice today.

Opposite: An example of Catherine the Great's Frog Setting with scenes of the English countryside

Maker's Marks

Josiah Wedgwood took a lesson from the British East India Company and became one of the first potters to consistently mark his wares and to advertise the mark. Records suggest he may have done this as early as 1759.

Over 250 years after Wedgwood's introduction of a Maker's Mark to support his brand, Steve Jobs also consistently demonstrated his critical support for a strong, recognizable, and approachable Apple identity in every element of brand communication.

Retail Showrooms

The first Wedgwood warehouse opened in London in 1765. Additionally, he was one of the first to market his products in full tabletop settings and to describe the vital importance of creating a unique retail experience.

> *"In the neatest, genteelest, and best method . . . a much greater variety of sets of vases should decorate the walls, and both these articles may, every few days be so altered, reversed and transformed, as to render the whole a brand-new scene."* —Josiah Wedgwood

> *"I need not tell you the many good effects this must produce, when . . . business and amusement can be made to go hand in hand."* —Josiah Wedgwood

The most perceptive element of this quote, and the one that would certainly appeal to Steve Jobs and every contemporary retailer, is the combination of business and amusement. Because at the beginning of the twenty-first century, in the context of technological advance, affluence, and cultural shifts, the service economy gave way to the experience economy.

By 1769, the Wedgwood showroom was one of London's most popular destinations, the Apple Store of its era. Wedgwood's competitors—including Boulton, Fothergill, Spode, and Mintonall—followed suit with their own London showrooms.

Wedgwood died in 1795 after a lifelong contribution to the evolution and growth of modern marketing. The brand he built still represents the characteristics of quality, innovation, and design over 225 years after his death.

Above and opposite: These two images of the Wedgwood showroom of the 1760s (above) and an Apple store in the 2020s (opposite) clearly demonstrate how the retail concept and merchandising layout was essentially identical, separated by over 250 years.

The Creation of Markets and Marketing

7

THE NEW RETAIL LANDSCAPE

Nineteenth-century technology radically transformed lifestyles. It was a time of increased worldwide prosperity and increased leisure time, where consumers were more able to focus on personal pleasures. During this time, three distinctly new retail forms emerged: the department store, the chain store, and mail-order merchants.

Economic and political power was shifting from monarchies to the manufacturers and merchants of the industrial revolution, from the landowner to the capitalist. Andrew Carnegie and Henry Frick dominated steel production. Jay Gould and Cornelius Vanderbilt ran the railroads. And John D. Rockefeller dominated the oil industry.

Cities continued their rapid growth, and families left the subsistence existence of the farm for employment in factories. As cities developed better sanitation, building codes, and food supplies, urban consumption grew, thus creating new demand for mass-produced products.

During this century, London grew from 1 million to 6.5 million residents. Incredibly, New York City exploded from 60,000 to 3.4 million people, growing over 560 percent.

It was also a time of massive and radical shifts in the way images were recorded, communicated, and distributed. Alois Senefelder and others developed mechanized lithographic printing, which was a quicker and cheaper process than engraving. The invention of photography replaced Marcantonio Raimondi's three-hundred-year-old system of cross-hatching as the primary method of rendering light and shadow. And John Calvin Moss's 1863 invention of photo engraving—later supplemented by half-tone reproduction—allowed photographs to be printed in mass quantities.

American history professor William Leach, in *Land of Desire*, talks about post-Civil War America and the creation of a more secular business- and market-oriented culture: "The features of this culture were acquisition and consumption as a means of achieving happiness, the cult of the new, and the democratization of desire . . . and money value as the predominant measure of all value in society."

Leach mentions that for the first half of the nineteenth century, most American white men were self-employed, property owners, and producers of foodstuffs and raw materials for a prosperous Atlantic trade. Largely free from the dangers of manufacturing that relied on a disciplined and dependent workforce to churn out goods, Americans rejoiced in their widely acquired prosperity.

Above: Philadelphia's Centennial Exhibition of 1876

As Leach points out, during the latter part of the century, an evolving consumer capitalist culture evolved with the emergence of three trends.

Development of a New Commercial Aesthetic

Leach maintains that "cultures must generate some conception of paradise or some imaginative notion of what constitutes a good life." He proposes that the heart of this new commercial aesthetic was "the visual materials of desire . . . color, glass, and light," all of which were evolving in a dramatic fashion during this century, thus putting the building blocks of modern marketing in place.

Philadelphia's Centennial Exhibition of 1876, the first world's fair in the United States—officially called the International Exhibition of Arts, Manufactures, and Products of the Soil and Mine—is a classic example of the promotion of this expanding commercial presence. At the time, the Exhibition's Main Hall was the largest building in the world, with over thirteen thousand exhibitors from thirty-seven countries.

Collaboration among Economic and Noneconomic Institutions

The economic expansion of the late nineteenth century was enabled by the coordinated efforts of a diverse range of organizations, including national corporations, department stores, investment banks, hotel chains, and the entertainment industry, as well as the Metropolitan Museum of Art, Harvard Business School, Wharton and Cornell universities, New York School of Design, and labor unions.

A New Class of Brokers

The new methodologies of communication and retail were the result of manufacturers' desire to sell even more products. Over time, display and decoration, advertising and promotion, fashion and style, and various modes of retail service were perfected.

As a result, US and European economies acquired a new commercial aesthetic driven by leading figures in the brokering class and institutional cooperation—leading to mass production, mass consumer institutions, and mass consumer enticements. This new mass marketing of products and services redefined the contemporary consumer lifestyle.

As the market for goods increased, three new retail formats served shoppers in new ways across urban and rural markets.

The Department Store—The Beginnings of Mass Retail

Developed in the early nineteenth century, the department store met both the qualitative and quantitative needs of urban retail growth. As Susan Strasser points out in *Satisfaction Guaranteed*, the department store had several unique aspects that clearly established a new relationship between the shopper and merchant.

The department store set fixed prices—at levels that would move merchandise—and allowed the shopper to both browse without buying as well as buy on credit. The creation of unique departments as separate profit centers within the stores improved record keeping so unprofitable ones could be dropped. While this practice of culling may have been practiced previously in retail, the scale of the department store brought efficiency.

These stores also had three new critical back-office methodologies: distribution systems capable of handling a large flow of merchandise, purchasing directly from the manufacturer, and buying large quantities for concessions on price and quality.

Opposite top left: The A. T. Stewart's department store

Opposite top right: An early A&P storefront

Opposite bottom: In Piggly Wiggly's aisles, for the first time, shoppers could see, touch, and read the packages and make informed choices without the assistance or interference of retail clerks.

Above: The 1908 Sears & Roebuck catalog

A. T. Stewart, built in New York City in the 1820s, was an early department store. It gradually expanded, and by 1862, the eight-story Marble Palace covered a city block at Broadway and Chambers Streets. The store was surrounded by white marble Corinthian columns, illuminated with gas light, and had hundreds of glass windows. Sixty thousand customers a day shopped at the store, served by one thousand clerks.

Department stores followed the northward residential expansion of Manhattan. Siegel & Cooper arrived on what was called Ladies' Mile in 1896, with a Beaux-Arts building at Sixth Avenue and Eighteenth Street. Leach describes it as "a steel framed stone building, 6 stories high, topped by a giant greenhouse, a roof-garden restaurant, a 200-foot tower."

One hundred and fifty thousand people attended the opening of this "shopping resort." The store planned for one hundred ninety thousand visitors a day and employed eight thousand clerks and one thousand drivers and packers. It had a telegraph office, a long-distance telephone office, a foreign-money exchange, stock-trading services, a dentist, and an in-house advertising agency.

Historian Neil Harris called these new store formats "mass encounters with the art and objects of the modern world; dramatic, persuasive, self-consciously designed to produce maximum effect."

The Mail-Order House

Even the largest of the department stores remained regional and primarily catered to an urban customer base. Before 1920, when car ownership allowed customers to easily get to the city, most rural shoppers were aware of these retailers only through their catalogs.

The most widely recognized catalog was Sears & Roebuck. In 1888, Richard Sears and Alvah Roebuck began with a small mailer for jewelry and watches. By 1895, the catalog had expanded to 532 pages of products.

Its Merchandise Building, built in 1906 in Chicago, sat on forty acres of land and contained a massive infrastructure, including a clothing factory, sixty-car railroad trains, a twenty-four-hour staff of over two thousand people opening nine hundred mailbags a day, a shipping company, a telegraph company, a post office, and a printing plant— all run by the second-largest power plant in Chicago.

The Chain Store: The Great Atlantic & Pacific Tea Company

Chain stores used new techniques of mass merchandising to create a third type of retail platform. The Great Atlantic & Pacific Tea Company, now known as A&P, was the most successful in this format. Starting in

1859 on Vesey Street in Manhattan selling teas, coffees, and spices, it used five innovative retailing tools in the expansion of its offerings. All these tools continue to be used by chain store retailers in both brick-and-mortar and digital store formats.

NATIONAL GROWTH PLAN

The company opened its first grocery store in 1912. Its growth plan relied on replacing the mom-and-pop stores of the time with a dramatically new store format. The first stores had no credit lines, no telephones, limited hours, and no delivery options, and were often located on back streets instead of main streets. What it did have was lower prices. This formula to sell groceries cheaper than the competition was a huge success.

A&P became the largest retailer in the world in only eight years. By the 1930s, with the stores expanding in size and selection, it was the largest food store chain with over 16,000 stores. Today, Kroger, the largest food retailer in the US, has about 2,750, while Walmart has 10,500 globally.

PRIVATE-BRAND PRODUCTS

A&P developed its own branded products, available only in its stores, in a number of categories. Baking powder was the first product in 1880, and these brands eventually included Sunnyfield, Sultana, Ann Page, and others.

LOYALTY PROGRAMS

It became the first chain store with customer savings and loyalty programs. These programs allowed shoppers to save on current purchases while also building up store credits that could be used in the future for retail discounts.

TRAVELING SALES AND DELIVERY FORCE

A salesforce of five to twenty salespeople working out of each store would travel locally and sell merchandise on commission.

A TIERED APPROACH TO RETAIL PLATFORMS

A&P explored different price points for retail categories throughout the store. This allowed it to appeal to a wide range of customer preferences and appeal to groups with different budgets. The 1920s coffee aisle was one example of this tiered approach. A&P sold three levels of price and quality: Eight O'Clock was its largest seller, Bokar was positioned as the premium brand, and Red Circle was the mid-level brand.

The Chain Store: Piggly Wiggly

Piggly Wiggly, the first self-service grocery store, was a radical transformation in grocery retail and ushered in what will be later described as "Retail 3.0."

The chain first opened in Memphis on September 6, 1916. Founder Clarence Saunders developed this self-service format in part because of the labor shortages of World War I and received a patent on the idea the following year.

At the time, grocery stores did not allow customers to hand-select their items. Instead, they would give a list of items to a clerk, who would then collect them throughout the store. This created more costs for the retailer, higher prices, and less opportunity for shoppers' choice.

Clearly the consumer's new ability to make personal shopping decisions while in the grocery store—what A. G. Lafley (chairman, president, and CEO of Procter & Gamble) described in 2005 as "the first moment of truth"—has in the intervening century led to the evolution of retail packaging and its role as the primary vehicle of brand identity.

Today's consumers, retailers, manufacturers, and brands rely on a modern omni-channel infrastructure offering a mix of traditional brick-and-mortar self-service stores and digital shopping experiences providing store pickup and home delivery. This infrastructure developed with Macy's, Sears, A&P, and Piggly Wiggly. These new retail formats offered customers new types of choices in when, where, and how they selected and purchased products, and these new opportunities for choice ultimately influenced the modern brand conversation that we take part in today every time we shop.

8

THE NEW MEDIA LANDSCAPE

As in the retail landscape discussed previously, the second half of the nineteenth century witnessed a radical transformation in the media landscape. The new imagery, content, and production values of this time echo throughout the influence and ubiquity of promotional media in popular culture today.

During this period, an increasingly complex media environment led to a rich new mosaic of brand-building and brand-promotion

opportunities. But first we must remember that the art of promotion has a long and storied past.

Li Bai (701–762 CE), a Tang Dynasty poet, may have written one of the first poem advertisements.

> *The wine of Lanling is full of the fragrance of tulips.*
>
> *The wine in the jade bowl reflects the color of amber.*
>
> *It helps the host to fully entertain his guests,*
>
> *making them lose their way home.*

Other early historical examples of advertising and brand promotion include political graffiti excavated in Pompeii, dating from just before the city was destroyed by the eruption of Mount Vesuvius in 79 BCE. Glassware traded throughout the Mediterranean world was created by Ennion, a first-century Roman craftsman who signed each piece in the mold with his identifying logo.

Importantly, the second half of the nineteenth century saw an unprecedented profusion of new visual media like photography, the lithographic poster, retail packaging, painted billboards, electrical signs,

---

Above: Retail packages of the nineteenth century

Opposite: The evolution of printing and design through the nineteenth century from 1818 on the left to the 1890s on the right

and the retail show window, all reflecting global changes in trade, culture, and technology.

As William Leach says of this time in *Land of Desire*, "Features of this culture were acquisition and consumption as the means of achieving happiness, the cult of the new, and . . . the democratization of desire."

To describe the visual excitement that this new media landscape inspired Artemus Ward, a nineteenth century American author and humorist, passionately characterizes this environment by saying "the grain, the texture, the juiciness, the savoriness, imprints on the buying memory . . . and speaks the universal picture language."

The Retail Package

By the late nineteenth century, the retail package was going far beyond the utilitarian purpose of product protection, becoming the standard communications vehicle for a rising number of national retail brands. In addition to its consistent presence in advertising, the package was the visual expression of brand identity and a major contributor to long-term brand equity.

Glass Bottles

The end of the nineteenth century saw a series of production advances in glass bottles. Beginning with simple blow molding by hand, semi-automatic machines arrived in 1898, followed by the Owens automatic bottle machine in 1905 and feed and flow machines in 1917. These technical advances allowed for significant growth in the availability of glass containers and an equally significant reduction in their cost. By the early twentieth century, 90 percent of the bottle production process was automated.

Folding Boxes

Mass production radically altered the economics of box manufacturing and use. Until the mid 1800s, boxes sold at retail were typically custom made for gifts and finished by hand. Robert Gair developed the process for the mass production of cartons in 1879, and in 1897, Uneeda Biscuit became the first large company to adopt the technology.

Tin Cans

English merchant Peter Durand developed a food and beverage preservation method using the tin can and received a patent in 1810. In subsequent years, the production and use of tin cans went through a series of innovations.

- 1846—Henry Evans invents a machine that can manufacture sixty tin cans per hour.

- 1858—Ezra Warner invents the can opener.

- 1866—J. Osterhoudt patents the can with a key opener, as seen on sardine cans.

- 1870—30 million cans a year are produced.

- 1906—The American Can Company is making 90 percent of cans in the US.

- 1920s—Charles Arthur Bunker invents the rotary opener.

Advertising Covers

In reality the first junk mail, these cards were mailed to potential customers and used regularly by advertisers in the late nineteenth century. This medium became one of the first ways to directly reach an audience in their homes with a visual message incorporating a brand's graphics.

Advertising Trade Cards

Essentially a small poster, this new media emerged in the 1880s and 1890s as one of the first vehicles combining the new visual tools of offset lithography with illustration. Colorful and amusing, they were distributed in a number of ways including at retail, by traveling salespeople, and at fairs and expositions.

Street Signage

Advertising and marketing transformed dramatically by the end of the century, from simple merchant signs to multistory illuminated electric signs. Stores and billboards were illuminated with new varieties of light, including gaslight, arc light, prismatic light, tungsten light, floodlights, and spotlights.

Display Windows

The shopping experience, from small-town Main Streets to Manhattan's Fifth Avenue, changed as well. The store window became the "medium" through which a retailer could present products in a visually exciting way that could be regularly changed for specific events, for holidays, or simply to display the latest merchandise.

The journalist Theodore Dreiser captured this spirit in the spring of 1905 while describing Fifth Avenue shop windows: "What a stinging, quivering zest they display, stirring up in onlookers a desire to secure but a part of what they see, the taste of a vibrating presence."

Writer Edna Ferber conjured up Greek mythology in 1911 when she described these environments and the bounty displayed behind the glass: "A breeder of anarchism, a destroyer of contentment, a second feast of Tantalus. It boasts peaches, downy and golden, when peaches have no right to be, strawberries glow therein when shortcake is last summer's memory."

And the retailer John Wanamaker used hundreds of windows in his New York and Philadelphia stores, saying, "Windows are eyes to meet our eyes."

Store Interiors

Retail interiors were becoming extraordinarily grand. The five-story atrium at Wanamaker's in Philadelphia featured the largest pipe organ in the world. With 28,750 pipes, it is still played twice a day and is a registered national historic landmark.

Photography

As the new medium of photography spread, the visual image began to supplant the written word. As one marketer of the period said, "You may forget what you read—if you read at all. But what you see, you know instantly."

Illustrations

This was the beginning of what became known as the "golden age of illustration." Complex images by illustrators like Howard Pyle, Jessie Willcox Smith, Charles Dana Gibson, Aubrey Beardsley, and J. C. Leyendecker all contributed lush visual support in advertising and brand building.

New Advertising Specialists

By the end of the nineteenth century, cohesive brand advertising had been present for several centuries—in spite of its questionable reputation. William Leach observes that before the 1880s, visual advertising was still looked down upon, often "linked to circuses and P.T. Barnum hokum."

The few advertising agents in the market were primarily space brokers, not content creators. Gradually, a new advertising industry attracted talented people like Elbert Hubbard, Maxfield Parrish, Helen Lansdowne, and window design and display artist L. Frank Baum, who later wrote *The Wonderful Wizard of Oz*.

One of the most prominent artists of the time was Maxfield Parrish. His painting *Daybreak*, inspired by the landscape of Vermont, is considered

Opposite: A can label of Butterfly Brand Beans (left) and Larkin Soap late-nineteenth-century trade cards (right)

the most popular art print of the twentieth century. The National Museum of American Illustration maintains it has outsold Andy Warhol's *Campbell's Soup Cans* and da Vinci's *Last Supper* and is still in print.

By 1910, Leach notes that these new mass marketeers "helped change not only the way many people saw and understood goods but also how they lived in their society."

Elbert Hubbard epitomizes this new attitude toward advertising. At age sixteen, he joined his brother-in-law selling Larkin Soap, then moved to the company's headquarters at nineteen. There he developed unique marketing and promotional ideas like gift-with-purchase promotions and consistent marketing slogans. Hubbard described the brand value of advertising, saying, "The things that live are the things that are well advertised. . . . To let the rogues and fools expound and explain you to the multitude, and you yourself make no sign, is to allow the falsehood to pass as current coin. It is not the thing itself that lives . . . it is what is said about it. So the moral is you must advertise, no matter how successful you are."

9

THE POSTER AS BRAND BUILDER

While the previously described changes in retail markets, media, and technology transformed the poster's supporting role in relation to brands, this form of media is deeply imbedded in the long and complex evolution of human expression, connection, and cultural communication.

Predecessors of the Poster (40,000 BCE–1789)

For tens of thousands of years, wall art—drawings, mosaics, frescos, and so on—was one of the only ways to publicly record the divine and the everyday. For millennia we have reached out to both communicate and leave our mark in a fashion that is very similar to what's being done today with social media.

The earliest examples of public human communication are found in several cave complexes—from around essentially the same time and at opposite ends of the world—including the Lubang Jeriji Saléh cave complex on Borneo and the Chauvet cave in France.

In the ancient civilizations of Mesopotamia, Egypt, and Greece, wall art also played a role in decoration, documentation, and literacy.

Today, the poster—with its modest cost, creative printing options, and placement flexibility—has largely replaced wall art for brand communication.

The Bastille to Industrial Wonders (1789–1848)

New printing technologies transformed what had been simple wall art expressions into paper-based posters that were applied to any public surface.

Opposite top left: Absinthe poster illustrated by Leonetto Cappiello

Opposite top right: Poster from the French Revolution

Opposite bottom left: Theater poster illustrated by Toulouse-Lautrec

Opposite bottom right: Politics, with Benjamin Franklin's 1754 poster, was served by posters.

MAURIN QUINA
LE PUY   FRANCE

1OULIN ROUGE   BAL
OULIN ROUGE   TOUS LES SOIRS
LA GOULUE

TERREUR   N. LAVEAU

UNITÉ
INDIVISIBILITÉ
DE LA
RÉPUBLIQUE
LIBERTÉ
ÉGALITÉ
FRATERNITÉ
OU LA
MORT

JOIN, or DIE.

In eighteenth- and nineteenth-century Europe, posters became political and commercial tools of revolution, with the French Revolution in 1789 followed by uprisings in Vienna, Milan, Berlin, Prague, Budapest, and Rome in the subsequent sixty years. The middle class was rising, the fashion and beauty industries were expanding, and the industrial and manufacturing revolution was changing the world.

The Poster's Golden Age (1848–1900)

The late nineteenth to the early twentieth century is considered the poster's golden age. This was partially due to new color offset printing technologies and prominent and talented illustrators who were attracted to the medium.

This extraordinary breadth of work is best demonstrated with examples of four very different product types: industry, live entertainment, absinthe, and the bicycle.

INDUSTRY

The poster was not just a retail consumer media. It also became a critical business-to-business communications vehicle for the industrial revolution and was used to promote a broad range of manufacturing and service companies.

THE THEATER

The cabaret and opera house were some of the most popular art forms of the time, and a new live entertainment/performance culture was emerging. With the invention of lithographic printing, theater managers realized that they could advertise their productions with brightly colored illustrations. Jules Chéret and Henri de Toulouse-Lautrec were the two most prominent poster artists of the time.

Eugène Grasset was another influential graphic artist who played an important role in the gradual transition from Victorian graphics to the art nouveau style.

ABSINTHE

Absinthe is an alcoholic botanical spirit made from wormwood, green anise, and sweet fennel. Due to the natural green color, the spirit is commonly referred to as *la fée verte* (the green fairy). Because of its popularity among radical artists and intellectuals, absinthe was vilified as the cause of unconventional ideas and a threat to the established order. Regardless, absinthe consumption in France in 1875 totaled 185,000 gallons. By 1910, that figure had increased to an astonishing 9,500,000 gallons.

THE BICYCLE

The modern bicycle was patented in 1866 and almost immediately became a favorite subject of poster marketing. And women became a critical consumer target. As Susan B. Anthony emphasized in 1896, "The bicycle has done more to emancipate women than any one thing in the world. I rejoice every time I see a woman ride by on a bike. It gives her a feeling of self-reliance and independence the moment she takes her seat; and away she goes, the picture of untrammeled womanhood."

End of the Belle Époque (1900–1914)

By the end of the nineteenth century, industry, technology, and prosperity had ushered in an explosion of lifestyle choices. Automobiles were, by 1900, a significant force in a changing mobile culture. Poster art reflected this new era of freedom and mobility.

The car begins to be shown as the only way to enter the future in style. In a 1914 advertisement for Mercedes, Ludwig Hohlwein portrays the state-of-the-art vehicle as the key to a charmed lifestyle. Gerold Hunziker uses a dramatic angle and unexpected colors to depict the front of a Bugatti Type 55 Roadster. The poster emphasizes newness: new designs, new technologies, and new experiences.

Lucian Bernhard entered a poster contest for Priester matches in 1905, and the result was revolutionary. After creating a number of more complex iterations, his entry was simply an image of matches on a bare dark field, with no distractions from the subject.

Bernhard was posthumously given the 1997 American Institute of Graphic Arts (AIGA) Medalist Award, where about this poster they enthusiastically said, "The Priester Match poster, by Lucian Bernhard, is a watershed document of modern graphic design. Its composition is so stark and its colors so startling that it captures the viewer's eye in an instant. Before 1905, when the poster first appeared on the streets of Berlin, persuasive simplicity was a rare thing in most advertising: posters, especially tended to be wordy and ornate."

Bernhard used this approach in next two decades of his career. His influence on German poster art would eventually become equally significant in American advertising and marketing.

War and Revolution (1914–1920)

The First and Second World Wars had a dramatic influence on culture and how ideas were portrayed.

Above: Priester matches poster by Lucian Bernhard

Opposite top left: Bicycle poster illustrated by Georges Massias

Opposite top right: Automotive poster illustrated by Gerold Hunziker

Opposite bottom left: This twentieth-century war poster featured stark images and reductive language.

Opposite bottom right: World War II propaganda produced a new series of visual icons, including the character Rosie the Riveter, featured in this "We Can Do It!" poster by J. Howard Miller.

The Depression of the 1930s generated a variety of posters, some simple and some richly decorative. Many were sponsored as part of the US government's Works Progress Administration.

The time between the wars was one of celebration, deep political concern, and political upheaval. Travel became more common, convenient, and accessible during the 1920s. Film was the new entertainment growth industry.

Metropolis, a 1927 German expressionist drama directed by Fritz Lang, is regarded as a pioneering science-fiction movie and among the first feature-length movies of that genre. With thirty thousand extras, its filming took place over seventeen months in 1925 to 1926 at a cost of more than five million Reichsmarks, or about $22 million USD today.

A Consumer Society (1945–1970)

Post-World War II consumer culture witnessed an explosion of words and images across a wide variety of styles and media, while brands targeted increasingly diverse audiences.

From its inception, the poster has been a unique medium for brands. With its modest investment, flexible placement opportunities, and unlimited imagery options, posters have enabled brands to create customized promotional plans for increasingly fragmented markets. This was especially true during the second half of the twentieth century. With its inherent flexibility, the poster offered brands the unique opportunity to take advantage of the new marketing tool of market segmentation. Additionally, it was able to be culturally adjusted for local markets.

Robert McGinnis was one of the most prolific and influential midcentury commercial artists. During the late midcentury period, his 1,400-plus movie posters, paperback covers, and magazine work embodied and influenced pop culture's liberated visual style.

Saul Bass, an AIGA medalist, created an iconic poster for *West Side Story*, which opened on October 18, 1961.

Opposite: Victor Moscoso studied art at Cooper Union in New York City and at Yale University and moved to San Francisco in 1959. Moscoso's use of vibrating Day-Glo colors was influenced by the painter Josef Albers, one of his teachers at Yale.

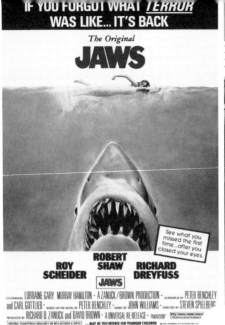

Fragmentation and Uniformity (1970–2000)

As brands continued to increase their cultural significance, the end
of the twentieth century witnessed the continued exploration of the
interplay between words and images. During this time, as the definition of "brand" continued to expand beyond traditional consumer
markets and into areas of public health, transportation, and politics,
the flexibility and consumer segmentation capabilities of the medium
saw the poster becoming an iconic brand communications vehicle that
contained some of the most memorable imagery of the period.

Roger Kastel created a poster for *Jaws*, the prototypical summer block-
buster, regarded as a watershed moment in motion picture history.
With its exploitation of deep psychological fears, it was the first film to
earn over $100 million USD at the box office.

Keith Haring's "Crack Is Wack" is perhaps his most legendary work.
The billboard's location in Manhattan on the busy Harlem River Drive,
next to passing cars, made it more visible than any other poster in the
city. It is an example of street culture, through placement and high
visibility, entering the mainstream. The Silence=Death Project was a
six-person collective in New York City. In 1987, the group produced

Above: The *Jaws* poster and Keith Haring's Crack Is Wack billboard

Opposite: Paula Scher's poster for Public Theater and the Shepard
Fairey poster for Obama

an iconic political poster, originally intended to be put up around New York City. Designed by Avram Finkelstein, the poster was used by the newly formed group ACT UP as a central image in its activist campaign against the AIDS epidemic.

This image is a contemporary example of brand as agitprop, or the use of popular media, such as literature, plays, pamphlets, and film, with an explicitly political message. But this is not unique to contemporary culture. As you have seen, almost from its inception, the poster has been used as a vehicle for cultural and political content.

As a Pentagram Partner, Paula Scher has managed the Public Theater's identity since 1994, a program that would go on to influence much of the graphic design created for theatrical promotion. The original identity for Savion Glover's "Bring in 'Da Noise, Bring in 'Da Funk" responded to the Public's mission to provide accessible and innovative performances, creating a graphic language that is almost graffiti-like. As with the Keith Haring's "Crack Is Wack" billboard, this is street culture becoming more mainstream.

Personal Expression (2000–2024)

The "Hope" poster was created in one day and printed first as a street poster. This piece became a seminal visual representation of his presidential campaign and continues to convey a clear and simple message. The image also represents a contemporary expression of the long-standing tradition of individuals-as-brand.

In closing, the connection between cave wall art and the contemporary poster has always been a very human drive to say, "I exist." But now with cheap and easy methods of reproduction (Xerox, Risograph, etc.), the poster has never been a more accessible medium for self-expression.

The poster remains a unique cultural medium, from the divinely personal to the simply promotional. Through the millennia, it has continued to play a significant role in the growth of brands . . . and how both visual and verbal expression is used to support them.

10

THE NAME ON THE LABEL (1900s)

In the early twentieth century, the old-world order gave way to a modern culture driven by industry, invention, entertainment, and consumer brands.

Continuous process manufacturing, an idea used for flour milling for over a century, was now critical for the mass production of most consumer packaged goods, including packed meat, brewed beer, canned vegetables, soap, cigarettes, matches, and breakfast cereals. As factories were adopting this process, new mass-marketing techniques emerged.

A 1900 quote from Artemas Ward—copywriter, member of the Advertising Hall of Fame, and editor of advertising trade magazines— hints at this move toward mass-market brands: "It is wonderful to note the volume of packages trading. . . . Nobody ever thinks of buying liquors or wines except in bottles showing where they come from, and who is responsible for their condition and character. . . . There has been a revolution in the last 20 years."

A customer had a few exceptions with national brands; typically, if a package had a mark, it was often from the wholesaler or retailer, not the manufacturer. At the turn of the century, most people still bought unbranded commodity products in bulk from small groceries and general stores.

Typical late-nineteenth-century product conversations appeared first between the manufacturer and the wholesaler, then spread to the wholesaler and the retailer, and finally occurred between the retailer and the consumer.

The development of brands, and the retail packaging that supported them, altered the balance of power. Manufacturers were now talking directly to the consumer, and brands were the topic of these conversations. As Susan Strasser mentions in *Satisfaction Guaranteed*, "Brands, as we know them today, would have no reason to exist without a direct conversation. Brands became the language of commerce—the new nouns in the marketing conversation."

There were nine emerging trends that drove the conversation.

Consumers Began to Ask for Brands

Brands were the way manufacturers controlled the retail and distribution process and leveraged distributors and retailers. Consumers no longer relied on the grocer's opinion about the best soap.

The Package's Physical Structure Was a Reassurance of Quality

Manufacturers used new packaging technologies that redefined consumer needs for safety, security, and sanitation. The "In-er-seal" carton from the National Biscuit Company, patented in 1899, was one of the first packages to reduce these fears and gain a competitive advantage.

The Trademark Act of 1870

In the late nineteenth century, there was a global movement to standardize the use and protection of brand trademarks.

The earliest European trademark legislation was the British Baker's Marking Law of 1266, which required all bakers to put a mark on the bread they baked. France passed its first comprehensive trademark law in 1857, and the United Kingdom followed with a Trademark Registration Act in 1875. Japan also enacted its first modern trademark act in 1884.

In 1870, American manufacturers gained the ability to protect unique design elements. The 1870 act established trademarks as the prima facie evidence of ownership; registered all marks in use for ten years or more; allowed for the destruction of infringing labels, and recovery of damages for infringement; prevented the importation of infringing goods; and allowed ownership forever. Under this act, an American trademark does not expire.

The Package Became Part of the Unique Selling Proposition

For brands like Colgate's Ribbon Dental Cream, where the paste is dispensed through a ribbon-shaped tube orifice, the package's aesthetics and tube structure become a critical part of the brand identity.

The Package Now Played a Major Role in Advertising and Promotion

As magazine and newspaper advertising, illustrated catalogs, billboards, and self-service retail exploded, the package became the brand's visual identifier.

The Association with the Manufacturer and the Brand Was Established

A diversity of approaches to brand architecture was established and today remains a major strategic decision for marketers. The critical question was whether to use a consistent manufacturer brand identity or segment by product type and create brand names for each category.

Manufacturers like Schilling and Libby chose a strong corporate brand approach, with a package design remaining consistent for all products. Procter & Gamble created Naptha, Ivory, and Star —each design with a different level of corporate brand endorsement usage—thus allowing for price and budget-based product segmentation.

The Brand Trademark Was Seen as Having Measurable Value to the Manufacturer

Branded goods expanded dramatically in the early twentieth century. In 1911, American Tobacco Company trademarks were estimated to be worth $45 million USD out of the $227 million USD in total assets.

Opposite top left: When manufacturers began to speak directly to consumers, an image of the package took on a prominent role in advertising.

Opposite top right: Colgate ad for Ribbon Dental Cream

Opposite bottom: Uneeda Biscuit magazine ad

PURE
DELICIOUS
VEGETABLE
FAT

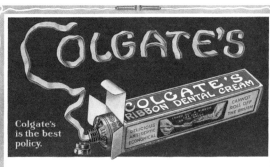

Brands Took on the Role of Cultural Education

As Strasser points out, "The creation of modern American consumer culture involved not only introducing new products and establishing market demand for them, but also . . . creating new domestic habits . . . People who had never purchased corn flakes were taught to need them. People who had always relied on photographers and barbers had to be told how to incorporate cameras and safety razors into their lives. And for Campbell's the problem was to sell the soup idea."

Kodak did groundbreaking work connecting consumers with photography's role in capturing modern life. As the company said, "Every man can write the outline of his own history, and that outline will be a hundredfold more interesting if it is illustrated." They were also one of the first brands to explore the Christmas opportunity by suggesting the camera as a gift as well as a method to record a family history.

Kodak was also one of the first marketers to understand the importance of becoming a "verb" in the brand conversation, much like Photoshop, Xerox, or Google in the twenty-first century.

The Media Targeted New and Larger Consumer Mass Markets

During this period, the role of advertising evolved from being just a source of information to an influence on lifestyle patterns, or from a cultural observer to a cultural influencer As a result, advertising's increased presence was felt across a variety of new and old media.

In the 1870s, *Godey's Lady's Book*, which accepted no advertising, was the leading women's magazine of the time, with a subscription price of $3 USD a year—the modern equivalent of $225 USD per year. *Ladies' Home Journal* took a new approach, which is still used by many contemporary media companies. It accepted advertising and then used those fees to reduce the subscription price to 50 cents. Within five years, the *Ladies' Home Journal* displayed more than twice as much advertising as any other woman's magazine and had millions of subscribers.

As competing newspaper publishers Joseph Pulitzer and William Randolph Hearst broadened their readership, the advertising in their papers moved toward the full-page layouts that still influence the look of modern print media.

Opposite top right: 1907 Kellogg's Corn Flakes advertisement

Opposite bottom left and right: These ads demonstrate Kodak's progressive approach to consumer education for product use and racial and gender parity.

"Excuse me—I know what I want, and I want what I asked for—**TOASTED CORN FLAKES** —Good day"

The package of the genuine bears this signature

W. K. Kellogg

TOASTED CORN FLAKES
W.K.Kellogg
TOASTED CORN FLAKE CO.
BATTLE CREEK, MICH.

A **KODAK** CHRISTMAS

Drawn for EASTMAN KODAK CO. by A. B. Frost.

There are no Game Laws for those who

Hunt with a Kodak

The rod or the gun may be left out, but no nature lover omits a Kodak from his camp outfit.

EASTMAN KODAK CO.

Rochester, N. Y.

Outside the home, new billboard companies advertised to the increasing number of car owners on the highways, with a guarantee of certain spaces for certain lengths of time.

Advertising agencies, which in the nineteenth century stuck to purchasing and brokering media space, now expanded their offerings to the creation of artwork, writing copy, market research, and managing product sampling and promotion.

Strasser notes that Charles Austin Bates, an early copywriting pioneer and ad agency founder, introduced the first example of the modern marketing and design brief in the 1890s, where he asked clients to fill out what he called a "symptom blank." This form gave the agency an introduction to the product, its history, and a definition of the client's interests in the services needed for the assignment.

As the offerings of the advertising industry increased, supported by a marked growth in new media avenues during this period, consumer brand's trust and reliance on the power of these services became more consistent. With the increase in new media opportunities, the critical rise in brand-building activities and an evolving consumer culture, we saw an advanced level of confidence in the link between advertising and commerce validating the growth of dramatic new brand-building opportunities in the consumer marketplace.

11

THE 1912 LAUNCH OF CRISCO—NEW PRODUCTS AND NEW LIFESTYLES

In 1912, after five years of intense research and development, Procter & Gamble launched Crisco, its first coordinated new brand introduction that incorporated the most sophisticated and integrated marketing tools and environments of their time, including consumer research, mass production, modern distribution infrastructure, a diverse retail marketplace, mass media, and advertising at scale.

The first advertisement for Crisco called it "An absolutely new product. A scientific discovery which will affect every kitchen in America. Something that the housewife has always needed."

Strasser notes that the marketing approach for Crisco is the result of a period of time—the forty years or so on either side of the turn of the twentieth century—when the United States had completed the transition from an agricultural to industrial society.

> *Crisco may be understood as an artifact of a culture in the making. A culture founded on new technologies and structured by new personal habits and new economic forms. . . . Americans everywhere and of all classes began to eat, drink, clean with, wear, and sit on products made in factories. Toothpaste, corn flakes, chewing gum, safety razors, and cameras, things nobody had ever made at home . . . provided the material basis for new habits and the physical expression of a break from earlier times. . . . A population accustomed to homemade products and unbranded merchandise . . . had to be converted into a national market for standardized, advertised, brand-named goods in general.*

The Crisco brand truly reflected the twentieth-century shift from an agricultural society to an industrial one, leading to a century of factory-produced food promotion. As one early Crisco ad proudly proclaimed, "Pure food from a clean factory. No kitchens can be so clean and wholesome as this factory."

Needless to say, this approach would not work today. In the early decades of the twenty-first century, consumers are increasingly searching for more wholesome and less processed food alternatives at all price levels. We are also witnessing a move from an industrial- and manufacturing-based economy to a more service-and experience-based one, which leads us to new food preferences and new lifestyle habits.

In April 1911, Procter & Gamble established the name and label design with the moon and stars logo. It then awarded the advertising account to J. Walter Thompson—its first outside agency. The Thompson office in Cincinnati was managed by Stanley Resor and his future wife, Helen Lansdowne. Together, they would later grow the agency into the largest of its time and the first to break $100 million USD in billings.

Helen Lansdowne wrote the opening campaign for Crisco, was the first woman to write and plan national advertising, and was among the first in the industry to adopt a number of innovations including an editorial writing style, celebrity endorsements, testimonials, free gift offers, and the use of sex appeal—specifically, images of men and women embracing. (She later became the first woman to be inducted into the Advertising Hall of Fame.)

Recognizing the power and flexibility of a key brand building, tool marketing, and sales promotion, Crisco's brand marketers explored seven or eight sales promotion plans, with each tested simultaneously. As Susan Strasser notes in *Satisfaction Guaranteed*, "In one city, they tried newspaper advertising; in another nothing but streetcar ads or outdoor posters or store demonstrations . . . In some cities, house to house canvassers, in others salesmen courted retailers."

Concurrently, the Procter & Gamble marketing staff worked on general analysis of the shortening market, investigating competition and developing product usage ideas.

In a brilliant promotional move, six cans of free product were sent to every grocer in America in December 1911, one month before the launch. The note to grocers said, "Sell the six cans and then order what further supply you need from your jobber."

This was followed by consumer ads, which mentioned that if they couldn't find Crisco at their local stores, they could order directly from Procter & Gamble for 25 cents and the name of their grocer.

By the end of 1915, *Saturday Evening Post* said, "Crisco is now a staple."

This free product giveaway was supported by national advertising, local grocery support with co-op ad programs, traveling demonstrators conducting week-long cooking schools throughout the US, and revised cookbooks with new recipes that were periodically mailed to consumers.

Market segmentation and product positioning techniques were developed and refined as part of this campaign. They ranged from consumer testing and product refinement to development of a national marketing strategy, with local variations, to product usage education in cookbooks and schools.

Packaging innovations included label and package variations for specific markets, an eight-page circle-shaped recipe booklet packed inside the lid of every can, a ten-pound container for railroad dining cars that was adopted by twenty-two railroads, and special packages bearing the seals of two rabbis, advertised in Yiddish media.

The Crisco campaign was so successful that J. George Frederick, the editor of *Printer's Ink*, said he thought it had established a unique methodology for new product introductions. "Instead of filling the earth and

Opposite top: The first Crisco retail package

Opposite bottom left: Early advertising for Crisco

Opposite bottom right: Early application of the Procter & Gamble moon and stars logo

the sky and all that therein is with flashes of publicity and grand hur-
rah," he felt Procter & Gamble "has in a final and authoritative manner
indicated the maximum efficiency method of marketing and finding
distribution for a new product."

Strasser notes that Crisco was one of the first brands that represented
a changing society open to national brands that were produced by
large consumer-product manufacturers. She notes, "As participants in
the branded mass market, consumers entered mutually dependent but
unequal relationships with large corporations."

12

PETER BEHRENS—BRAND IDENTITY AROUND THE WARS

One individual, with his prescient sense and clear understanding of
how and why to build coordinated and intently curated corporate
activities and appearances, was an articulate early practitioner in what
became known as corporate and brand identity.

As the twentieth century moved into its second decade, consumers'
brand relationships were continuing to develop in an increasingly
complex mix of choices in media, retailing, entertainment, lifestyle,
and product technologies. It was becoming clear that these relationships were influenced by every touchpoint that a brand possessed. In
the case of AEG (Allgemeine Elektricitäts Gesellschaft), the German
designer Peter Behrens recognized that its consumer-brand relationships were deeply influenced by a wide variety of touchpoints,
from the smallest elements of typography or a stationery system, to a
consistent aesthetic for product design, to the design of the largest and
most visible manufacturing facilities.

As these relationships became more complex, a few astute manufacturers were recognizing its importance. Behrens, with his holistic
approach to corporate and brand identity, was one of the earliest and
most adept practitioners to recognize the critical role of a crafted and
cohesive image in shaping this new consumer-brand relationship. This
was a significant event in corporate brand building.

Opposite: The new AEG logo supported consistently applied and
comprehensive print media.

Design and Consumption

Peter Behrens was born in 1868 in Hamburg, Germany, a city with a population that had quadrupled in the last half of the nineteenth century due to its role as Europe's third largest port. Hamburg was home to Europe's largest shipping line, and its Church of St. Nikolai was the tallest building in the world when Behrens was born.

When Behrens was fourteen, his father died, leaving him a substantial inheritance that afforded him economic independence. He painted for much of his early life until his late twenties, when he became interested in graphic design and the applied arts.

To give you a sense of his position in design history, Philip Meggs, a prominent design historian and biographer, describes Behrens's contributions this way: "He occupies a position in 20th-century design similar to the positions of Cezanne and Picasso in painting. . . . Behrens was a catalytic innovator whose work altered the course of design in this century."

Simply put, Behrens was one of the earliest and most consistently sensitive individuals who understood the symbiotic visual relationships that each element of an integrated design system must support. As a result, he redefined how a creative vision can transform corporate and brand image within a corporation. His integrated approach to design became the authoritative standard for designers that followed.

In creating this approach to a unified identity system, he was responsible for a number of firsts.

A First in Typography

The evolution of typography over time has been one of the historic design markers that identifies a creative era. Recognizing this, and feeling the need to reflect contemporary typography in his work, Behrens was the first to use sans serif text as running book text, as well as on the title and dedication pages in his 1900 booklet *Celebration of Life and Art: A Consideration of the Theater as the Highest Symbol of a Culture*, according to the German typographic historian Hans Loubier.

A year later, he explored geometric typographic motifs with sans serif characters based on the square. In 1904, he experimented with dramatic geometric forms based on the grid, rigid proportions, and geometries, suggesting the formalism to come with the Bauhaus.

Philip Meggs says his work during this time "represents a synthesis of two seemingly contradictory concepts . . . a careful study of the art and design of ancient Greece and Rome . . . and a pragmatic emphasis upon technology, manufacturing processes, and function."

Above and Opposite: Examples of product design philosophy that created work that was related with a uniquely styled aesthetic

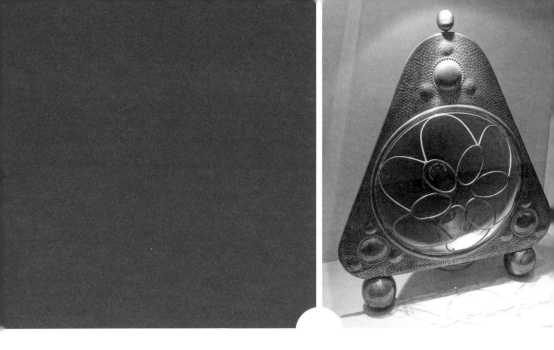

A First in Corporate Identity

In 1907, AEG hired Behrens as its first artistic adviser. As a designer, he was now in a place to develop a unified corporate identity program.

AEG was the German company that had bought the European manufacturing rights to Thomas Edison's patents in 1883. As a result, it had grown into one of the world's largest manufacturing companies.

This early twentieth-century synthesis of the classic and the modern, as described in the previous Meggs quote, informed Behrens's development of its identity system. A program much like those developed in the last half of the twentieth century.

- **Logo:** The AEG hexagonal trademark was designed in 1908 and was an intentional reference to the complexity of the company as a modern industrial beehive.

- **Typography:** Unique typography is a key element in the creation of a unique visual identity, and Behrens recognized that a bespoke typeface must be part of the integrated visual equity of the AEG brand. The typeface, called Behrens Antiqua, was designed for AEG's exclusive use. This face combined the inspiration of Roman brass work with modern geometry monumentalism.

- **Visual Identity System:** Printed materials were designed with a consistent appearance through the use of rules governing the placement of graphic elements, exclusive use of typography, analogous colors, and consistent approach to photography and drawings.

A First for Industrial Design

Behrens is credited with being the first modern industrial designer. A series of objects, from tea kettles, fans, streetlamps, and electric motors, had a consistent approach to design, materials, and production efficiencies.

His kettle was a model of both aesthetics and efficiency, with three basic forms, two lids, two handles, two bases, three materials, and three finishes. The elements allowed for the production of eighty-one different kettles from one design. This kettle was an early example of modular mass production, in which the design of a product supported two goals—choice for the consumer and profitable productivity for the manufacturer.

About this work, Meggs said, "Behrens stripped connotations of social class and wealth from these products. His work pointed toward a new sensibility about design, which matured in the 1920s . . . the need for form to emerge from function rather than being an added embellishment."

A First for Architecture

Behrens designed the AEG Turbine Hall between 1909 and 1912. He adapted the AEG corporate design philosophy by combining aesthetic elements of classic and contemporary architecture. This was a building that served two functions. First, it supported workers by creating a healthy, light-filled environment. And just as importantly, with its sensitive design, the building worked as an exemplar that supported the notion of AEG as a good neighbor. Behrens's identity system ranged from logos to products to buildings, culminating in a comprehensive corporate aesthetic—a significant historical event.

A First for Design Education

Perhaps his most important legacy was using the AEG brand to educate and inform people on how to live in the modern world. Behrens's

Opposite: The Turbine Hall, one of many buildings that had a specific architectural philosophy

work at AEG was a thesis for how the objects we create should be built and cultivated.

His program included a number of individuals who would later have an immeasurable impact on the future of design. As a result of this commitment, he began an apprentice program that included a key group of designers and architects who would go on to lead organizations like the Bauhaus and create some of the most iconic designs of the twentieth century. They include

- Walter Gropius, founder of the Bauhaus,

- Ludwig Mies van der Rohe, Bauhaus director and one of the pioneers of modern architecture,

- Le Corbusier, architect with seventeen projects listed as UNESCO World Heritage sites, and

- Adolf Meyer, Bauhaus Master who worked with Gropius.

Behrens understood that design not only represented the creation of a coherent and striking visual appearance. Like any brand-related corporate and creative discipline, it must also represent the past, present, and future of an organization. Therefore, it must be taught, nurtured by each succeeding generation, and have practitioners who understand how to promote and care for it.

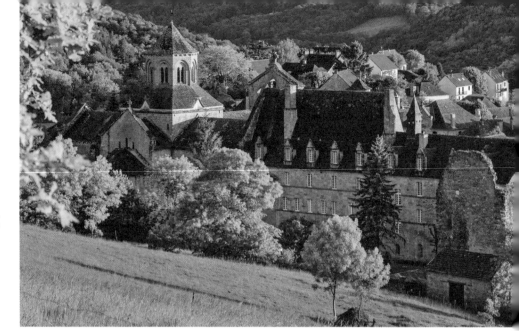

13

COCO CHANEL AND THE CREATION OF CHANEL NO. 5

At the beginning of the twentieth century, a scent of change was in the air. Coco Chanel caught that scent and channeled her unique child-hood, innate creativity, strong sense of purpose, and independence to create the most significant and largest-selling fragrance brand the world has ever seen.

Her background was labyrinthine, with each pathway adding com-plexity to her life. From a lost young girl in a harsh and isolated orphanage to a global fashion icon, her fragrance brand is a direct reflection of that complexity.

Virginia Woolf, the modernist writer, summed up the feeling of the time: "On or about December 1910 human character changed." She continues, "I am not saying that one went out, as one might into a garden, and there saw that a rose had flowered, or that a hen had laid

Above: The Abbey Church at Aubazine

Opposite: Coco Chanel in 1910

an egg. The change was not sudden and definite like that. But a change there was, nevertheless . . . in religion, conduct, politics, and literature."

You probably know some version of Chanel's life story: Gabrielle Bonheur Chanel was born out of wedlock in 1883, her mother died in 1895 when Coco was twelve, her father abandoned the family, and she and her brother entered a convent orphanage in the small country town of Aubazine in the Nouvelle-Aquitaine region of central France.

It was here she learned the lessons of independence and austere simplicity and where the sights and smells of rich summer gardens contrasted against the crisp cleanliness of the convent's scrubbed hallways and freshly laundered clothing.

This is the classic contrast of lushness with disciplined austerity that her fragrance, and her clothes, would become known for.

At eighteen, she moved to a small town, became a seamstress, explored singing and theater, became pregnant, had a botched abortion, and was for several years the "second" live-in mistress of Étienne Balsan, a dashing textile heir and army officer.

It was on the Balsan estate that she began her early lessons in fashion and fragrance, while making the important connections that would serve her well throughout her life: royalty, the well-born, and the creative class of artists, writers, musicians.

Mingling with men and women of all classes and backgrounds, she learned the secrets of scent and sensuality. Simply put, respectable women of the time wore the easily identifiable fragrances of a single flower, while women of the street wore rich, complex scents hinting at musk and desire. The division was well known.

Interest in fragrance was blooming. The Corsican fragrance entrepreneur François Coty had become one of France's wealthiest men. Paul Poiret became the first couturier to launch his signature scent, Nuit d'Perse, introduced during an extravagant all-night party at his Paris mansion on June 24, 1911. He gave each guest a small flacon of the scent as they left in the morning.

During this period, strict realism in the arts was seen as increasingly passé. Artists had been experimenting with impressionism for decades, and artists like Picasso, Leger, and Matisse worked almost exclusively with abstraction. Flowers were no longer just flowers, in the art world or in the world of fragrance.

While artists were beginning to represent the natural world with the cubist brush, fragrance houses and perfumers were exploring new scents using molecules invented by laboratory chemists. Aldehydes, first synthesized in the late nineteenth century, would revolutionize the fragrance world just as artists revolutionized the way we see a landscape, still life, or simple rose.

In the summer of 1920, Coco Chanel began working in earnest with perfumer Ernest Beaux. With the end of World War I, the Western world was struck by the notion of "the modern," which collided head-on with traditional images of femininity. With simpler silhouettes, more casual looks, and new fabrics like silk jersey, designers like Chanel were redefining women's fashion stereotypes leading into the 1920s.

As biographer Tilar Mazzeo says in *The Secret of Chanel No. 5*, "It is impossible to understand Chanel . . . except as part of this larger project of redefining twentieth-century femininity."

Chanel herself said, "Women are not flowers. Why should they want to smell like flowers? I want to give a woman an artificial perfume. Yes, I do mean artificial. A woman should smell like a woman, not like a flower."

After working through the summer, Beaux finally invited Chanel to test the fragrances. He set them out in a line of ten small identical glass

Opposite: Chanel No. 5 fragrance bottles one hundred years apart

"A drop of N°5, and nothing else."

N°5 AND MARILYN MONROE CHANEL OOM

vials, labeled 1 through 5 and 20 through 24. Each was a variation that contained scents of may rose, jasmine, and the new aldehydes. But surprisingly, a lab assistant had misread Beaux's notes and mistakenly added a massive overdose of aldehydes to one of the samples.

Mazzeo vividly describes the moment: "She slowly drew each sample beneath her nose . . . Her face revealed nothing. In one of those perfumes, something in the catalogue of her senses resonated, because she smiled and said, at last, with no indecision: 'Number 5.'"

Mazzeo goes on to describe Chanel's response to the fragrance and her complex connection to the number 5.

> Yes, that is what I was waiting for. A perfume like nothing else. A woman's perfume, with the scent of a woman.

> It was the memory of all her childhood scents and the mystery of numbers surrounding her at Aubazine.

> It had been Boy Capel's magic number, too, something they shared. The number five was a special part of theosophism . . . It was the number of quintessence . . . A fortuneteller had told her it was the number of her special destiny.

And Chanel told Beaux, "I present my dress collection on the fifth of May, the fifth month of the year, and so we will let this sample number five keep the name it has already, it will bring good luck."

Chanel No. 5 was a truly modern fragrance with two bouquets: one natural, the other synthetic. It reflected the combined sensual experiences of her childhood: the complex fragrance of the French countryside and the sterile, clean odors of the convent.

She initially marketed the fragrance in a stealthy way, simply by giving small bottles to her most loyal clients as holiday gifts in late 1920. Essentially igniting a whisper campaign to test the market in Paris, she claimed it was simply a little bottle of something she had picked up in Grasse and couldn't remember where she had found it.

The explosive success among the fashionable grew only by word of mouth. Advertising would not be part of the initial launch, and she sold it exclusively out of her shop for the first three years.

That all changed quickly in 1924, when she asked the brothers Pierre and Paul Wertheimer to help her build an international market for No. 5 and her other beauty and personal care products. They founded Société des Parfums Chanel with this aim.

Their very first brochure described the packaging in extraordinary terms that captured the scent's uniqueness:

> *The Chanel perfumes, created exclusively for connoisseurs, occupy a unique and unparalleled place in the kingdom of perfume. The perfection of the product forbids dressing it in the customary artifices. Why rely on the art of the glassmaker or the manufacturer of cartons! This so often brings an air of prestige to a dubious product and brings mercenary cheers from the press to sway a naive public.*
>
> *Mademoiselle Chanel is proud to present simple bottles adorned only by their whiteness, precious teardrops of perfume of incomparable quality, unique in composition . . . revealing the artistic personality of the creator.*

Since then, only very subtle changes to the bottle design have been introduced.

Chanel fragrances hit the American market in the 1920s, and business exploded. Sales of French perfumes in America increased more than 700 percent in the decade between 1919 and 1929. Yet Chanel's marketing and advertising remained surprisingly restrained.

So Chanel No. 5 remains the very opposite of the gaudy, art nouveau-inspired bottles that were typical for the time. Chanel No. 5's simple bottle has, of course, become an icon. It was a reflection of her life, an act of defiance, of simply saying no to tradition.

As Chanel herself said, "Elegance is refusal."

14

C. COLES PHILLIPS—AN ILLUSTRATOR'S DEFINITION OF THE TWENTIETH-CENTURY WOMAN

During the second and third decades of the twentieth century, North America was becoming a globally connected culture increasingly organized around, and driven by, mass communication, opening radical new ways for brands to reach consumers. Advertising was becoming a ubiquitous brand promotion tool, and its most visible practitioners— art directors, writers, photographers, and illustrators—were beginning to influence cultural norms.

C. Coles Phillips was one of the most prominent illustrators of the period, and his work had a powerful role in presenting and influencing bold, new, and idealized lifestyles and aesthetic tastes. Phillips and other producers of posters, newspapers, national magazines, and radio helped institutionalize and enable a more sophisticated and homogeneous society.

Importantly, Phillips updated the image of women from the Edwardian age into the twentieth century. His images were consistently more modern, active, and athletic images of women.

Born in Ohio in 1880, Phillips left for New York City in 1902 to earn a living as an illustrator. To pay the bills, Phillips worked as a clerk at the American Radiator company, where an unflattering caricature of the company's president cut short that position after only a few months.

The evening of his dismissal, the coworker for whom Phillips did the drawing was dining with J. A. Mitchell, the publisher of *Life* magazine. Upon hearing the story of dismissal, he asked to see the offending drawing, liked it, and asked that Phillips come by to see him.

He never went to the interview. Instead, Phillips enrolled in art classes, where he lasted three months.

Finally in 1907, Phillips decided it was time to take Mitchell up on his offer. He presented one image, carefully crafted to match the *Life* magazine style. It landed him the job at the age of twenty-six.

Later that year, Phillips created a cover that would become his trademark. By combining similarly colored foreground and background elements, he created the "Fadeaway Girl."

Above and Opposite: Magazine covers from 1915 and 1921 that illustrate Phillips's use of the "Fadeaway Girl" technique, where a flat one-color background acts as the visual foundation for the important details rendered in great full-color detail in the foreground

APRIL 7, 1921
VOL. 77

Life

Copyright, 1921, Life Publishing Company

PRICE 15 CENTS
NO. 2005

In a Position to Know

Within a few months, Phillips was competing with well-known illustrators like James Montgomery Flagg and Charles Allen Gilbert.

Phillips's work was such a success that he created over fifty-four cover paintings for *Life* magazine in the next four years—essentially one cover illustration every month. He also began working for other national magazines, including *Ladies' Home Journal. Good Housekeeping* asked him to paint a cover image every month for five years.

Given the prominence of these magazines during this period, it's more than likely that most consumers saw his cover illustrations either on a newsstand or in the home.

Just as there was a "Gibson girl" at the turn of the century, there was a "Phillips girl" in the teens and twenties. She showed a lot more skin than her older sister, but she still had a wholesome look. And over time, the decorum so prevalent prior to the war gave way to an overt sensuality, clearly seen in ads from 1917 to 1922 for Luxite Hosiery, Holeproof Hosiery, and Overland Auto.

Above: Luxite Hosiery ad from 1918

Opposite: Two early Jell-O ads (the left circa 1910 and the right from 1919) showing the significant difference in modern stylistic elements, including clothing, hairstyles, and architectural details

QUICK
EASY

JELL-O
TRADE MARK REG. U.S. PAT. OFF.

WONDER
DISHES

Entrées *Relishes* *Salads* *Desserts*

Some New Ideas

Shouts of "Oh, Good-e-e-e!" and clapping of hands greet mamma's appearance with a big dish of Jell-O for Bobbie and Jack.

It is a plain dish of Strawberry Jell-O, served without sugar or cream—but perfectly delicious. Ask the children—they know.

Substantial dishes that are good to eat and made without sugar, eggs or cream are very popular just now. Probably the Bavarian creams made after the recipe below are in all respects the most satisfactory of this particular style of dish.

Pineapple Bavarian Cream

Dissolve a package of Lemon Jell-O in a half-pint of boiling water and add half a pint of the juice from a can of pineapple. When cold and still liquid whip to consistency of whipped cream and add a cup of shredded or chopped pineapple.

Either fresh or canned fruit of almost any other kind can be used in making these Bavarian creams. Canned peaches and peach juice are particularly good.

Any flavor of Jell-O except Chocolate may be used for these Bavarian creams, but Lemon Jell-O is best for Pineapple Bavarian Cream.

The whipped Jell-O takes the place of whipped cream in these dishes, and neither sugar nor eggs are used in them.

And then there are salads—dozens of different kinds—that are as attractive and delightful in all respects as the Jell-O desserts are.

The new Jell-O book contains a special recipe for whipping Jell-O, which is a simple process. If you have not already received a copy of this 1918 Jell-O Book we shall be glad to send you one if you will give us your name and address.

Jell-O is put up in six pure fruit flavors: Strawberry, Raspberry, Lemon, Orange, Cherry, Chocolate, and is sold by all grocers, **2** packages for **25** cents.

THE GENESEE PURE FOOD COMPANY, Le Roy, N. Y., and Bridgeburg, Ont.

In a time of commercial artwork led by Alphonse Mucha and Maxfield Parrish, the most famous names in illustration, Phillips came up with a new approach to content and composition that reflected the changing times.

15

THE ROLE OF THE NEW CONSUMER

As the twentieth-century branded mass market grew, consumers were entering into mutually dependent, but unequal, relationships with large corporations.

In *Making a New Deal: Industrial Workers in Chicago*, Lizabeth Cohen argues that "working-class urban residents found an identity as Americans and as New Dealers as the result of their incorporation into a burgeoning mass culture."

She describes two types of consumers at this time. Citizen Consumers were "regarded as responsible for prodding government to protect the rights, safety and fair treatment of individual consumers in the private marketplace." Purchaser Consumers were "viewed as contributing to the larger society by exercising purchasing power rather than through asserting themselves politically."

Cohen confirms that the power of producers was typically thought to be the main economic driver leading up to the twentieth century. This view was significantly altered during the First Progressive Era of the late nineteenth and early twentieth century, which saw a movement against the increasing industrialization of the time.

Out of this "first wave" progressive movement came organizations like the National Consumers League, founded in 1899 by middle-class women who promoted "ethical consumption." Florence Kelley was the organization's founder and first general secretary, and her guiding principle lives to this day on the League website: "To live means to buy, to buy means to have power, to have power means to have responsibility."

Opposite: The first wave of the consumer movement, targeting the monopolies of the late nineteenth century, captured in this 1889 Puck political cartoon

The 1920s saw further advances in the production, distribution, and purchase of standardized goods. Most Americans at this time recognized the growing influence of mass consumption, yet not all participated equally. In 1930, there were more people lacking a washing machine, vacuum cleaner, radio, or car than people who had one.

By the end of the decade, consumers were not yet considered, as Cohen describes, "a self-conscious, identifiable interest group on par with labor and business."

That shift in mindset would not occur until the economic collapse of the Great Depression and the second-wave consumer movement it inspired. Cohen suggests that as the 1920s came to a close, the New Deal, instituted in the early 1930s by Franklin Delano Roosevelt to bring about immediate economic relief during the Depression, would institutionalize the rights of various constituencies, including the farmer, the laborer, and the small-business owner. And consumers' actions were now considered a means of enhancing the public's social stake in the economy while still preserving the free-enterprise system.

During the Depression, there was call for permanent consumer representation in government, which led to what Cohen describes as the "second-wave consumer movement." In a 1932 address, President Roosevelt said, "I believe we are at the threshold of a fundamental change in our popular economic thought, and that in the future we are going to think less about the producer and more about the consumer."

Roosevelt supported "a new principle in government" that consumers have the right to have their interests represented in the formulation

THIS IS THE
STOREKEEPER
HE SELLS THE THINGS THAT
ARE GOOD FOR YOU TO EAT
HE MUST KEEP THE FOOD CLEAN

of government policy, and consistently placed consumer advocates in various agencies. The Food, Drug, and Cosmetic Act of 1938 included some at-the-time radical requirements for brands, including expanding government jurisdiction to cosmetics and medical devices, new label requirements to prevent adulteration and misbranding, requiring drug manufacturers to prove product safety before marketing, and strengthening enforcement procedures against hazardous substances.

Women made up much of the rank-and-file membership of consumer movements during the 1930s. *Nation's Business*, the monthly magazine published by the Chamber of Commerce of the United States during that time, wrote,

> *Until recent years, the consumer movement was supposed to be nothing but a lot of ladies' bridge clubs meeting every Thursday and setting up committees to heckle the local advertisers and merchants. The Depression, however brought the consumer interest to the fore in the already organized women's organizations.*

As reflected in the *Nation's Business* quote, this new activism by women particularly troubled the traditionally conservative male business

Above: This New Deal poster, commissioned by government organizations including the Works Progress Administration, reflects a new government focus on the consumer movement in the 1930s.

Opposite: Women were the driving force in the meat boycotts, along with unions.

leaders. For example, newly empowered women's groups were a leading force in the meat boycotts, motivated primarily by the rising cost of meat and supported by a cohesive group of working-class housewives. These boycotts took place in 1935, with over ten thousand taking part in actions in Los Angeles, Detroit, New York, and Chicago.

African Americans also saw spending power as one of the few ways to influence government and industry. Their consumer-based protests of unequal business practices included the "Don't Buy Where You Can't Work" and "Spend Your Money Where You Can Work" movements. This newly recognized group had significant purchasing power in their communities and was passionately understood by leaders of the movement like W. E. B. Du Bois, who said, "Do not think the economic cycle begins with production, rather it begins with consumption."

Roosevelt supported the emergence of a new model of economics based on the critical importance of consumption, developed by John Maynard Keynes. Significantly for consumer brands, this economic model recognized the importance of consumption and stimulus at sensitive times of economic stress. Underconsumption was seen as one cause of the Great Depression, and that increased purchasing

Above: African Americans were a significant force in the mid-twentieth-century consumer movement, including Depression-era activities like a boycott of Bowman Dairy in Chicago or the "Don't Buy Where You Can't Work" protests in Berkeley, California.

power was the key to recovery. In his acceptance speech at the 1936 Democratic National Convention, Roosevelt said, "Today we stand committed to the proposition that freedom is not a half-and-half affair. If the average citizen is guaranteed equal opportunity in the polling place, he must have equal opportunity in the marketplace."

16

ALEX STEINWEISS AND PAUL RAND—TWO CREATIVE APPROACHES TO NEW BRAND MEDIA

As this book has noted, Josiah Wedgwood and Steve Jobs were merchants, separated by three centuries, who shared deeply held feelings about the nature, quality, and power of their brands.

In contrast, Alex Steinweiss and Paul Rand were designers, both practicing during the mid-twentieth century, who shared a common interest in applying a contemporary approach to elements of typography, illustration, color, and composition to create the visual definition of brands in two distinctly different areas of design practice.

Both were innovative practitioners who took their medium beyond the expectations and norms of their time, and both are still considered visionary master craftsmen. They grew up in working-class neighborhoods of Brooklyn during the 1920s and 1930s, attended Parsons School of Design, and began their careers in the late 1930s.

This is a story very typical of many New York graphic designers in the second half of the twentieth century. So, while their backgrounds may not be unique, what makes this story different is their extraordinary talent and that they each took advantage of a critical time and place in the twentieth-century collision of brands and modern creativity.

Steinweiss went to work for Columbia Records and became the first innovator of album cover artwork. This made him a transformational figure and the creator of an entirely new form of consumer package design and retail promotion. His work revolutionized the music business.

His empathy for the music, unique craftsmanship, and extraordinary creativity came together into a groundbreaking approach to visually describing the product: music on an album. This critical connection between the product and its representation on a retail package is a lesson still relevant to all consumer brand designers eighty-five years later.

Paul Rand, while he began as a publication designer for *Esquire* and *Direction* magazines, is best known as a leading modernist innovator of corporate brand identities. As his biographer Phil Meggs suggests, "Rand's contribution to modern graphic design theory in total is widely considered intrinsic to the profession's development."

Intriguingly, looking back at their careers, they both expressed an essential personal motivation to go beyond the safe expectations of the design field of the time.

In an interview with George Lois in 1986, Rand said, "I had the courage or the audacity or the stupidity to take a chance. I didn't know what the hell would happen."

Steinweiss, in *Alex Steinweiss: The Inventor of the Modern Record Cover* by Kevin Reagan, said, "I was willing to go way beyond what the hell they paid me for. I wanted people to look at the artwork and hear the music."

The vinyl record album has seen a resurgence in the market, perhaps reflecting an interest in both the analog nature of its sound as well as the resurgence of album graphics that visually reflect its content.

And unlike the printed corporate annual report, and other forms of print media, the album cover is not just a major vehicle for the brand expression of artists, writers, composers, and musicians of all types— it continues to be a great design medium.

As Steven Heller, designer, historian, and cofounder of the SVA Masters in Branding program, says in the introduction to Steinweiss's book, "Alex Steinweiss invented cover art for the record album. . . . He recognized a need and invented a genre that was as revolutionary in its way as sound was to film and color was to television. It added an entirely new dimension to the musical experience—and, not incidentally, the sale of recorded music."

Steinweiss was the first art director for CBS Records. In 1939, the record industry had no design tradition. Seventy-eight-rpm records were packaged in bulky boxes with three to four records each in a separate kraft-paper sleeve. Albums were often sold in appliance stores near the record players.

Steinweiss was hired to develop music promotion, ads, posters, booklets, and catalogs. After a few months, he suggested designing the

---

Opposite: The first album cover by Steinweiss in 1939

album covers and was allowed to experiment on a few titles. The first album was a collection of Rogers & Hart showtunes.

His work was certainly influenced by the bold poster graphics of the time, but it contained completely new ways of visually referencing the history, content, and spirit of the music. A visual lyricism was evident in the covers. Of an early Béla Bartók cover he said, "I took the elements of the piano—the hammers, keys, strings—composed them in a contemporary setting using appropriate color and rendering. Since Bartok was Hungarian, I also put in the suggestion of a peasant figure."

Heller adds, "As he matured, Steinweiss reveled in the fact that music stimulates the visual imagination far beyond the more conventional iconography with which he began his career."

As you look at this work, remember they were rendered by hand, with a brush, rapidograph pen, ruler, and airbrush. Most of this work was printed on two- to three-color letterpress presses. Steinweiss began with a miniature sketch and then developed a base layer for the artwork, added separate layers for each additional color, and hand separated the artwork as he created it.

In a 1947 interview in *American Artist*, he says of his work, "An album cover is designed, not merely to be a pretty picture. . . . The design elements are composed in a simple dynamic style and are chosen for their ability to convey to the onlooker enough about the nature of the music to arouse in him a longing."

In the mid-twentieth-century environment, especially in the immediate post-World War II era, corporate brand identity was coming under the influence of radically new cultural trends as diverse as abstract expressionist art, a heightened diversity in the expanding publishing and media landscapes, and the increasing sophistication of corporate brand management. Paul Rand was one of the few design practitioners with a clear and omniscient sense of the changing nature of the period. He thrived in this dynamic and led a movement that combined his interest in painting, photography, typography, color, abstraction, psychology, surrealism, and cultural movements such as Cubism and the Bauhaus.

Rand contributed to the corporate identity programs of companies like American Express, Cummins Engine, ABC, UPS, Enron, Morningstar, and NEXT Computer. His lifetime of work is best represented by the multifaceted and multimedia work for IBM, a client from 1956 until the late 1990s. This graphic design work was initially created in a strategic creative partnership with the architect and industrial designer Eliot Noyes, thereby creating a complete and synergistic identity program that followed in the early twentieth-century tradition of Peter Behrens at AEG.

But a judgment on Rand's influential body of work should not be limited to his corporate brand identity programs. His lifetime contributions to graphic design in the form of book covers, posters, and other forms of print were equally influential. Importantly, it is with this print work that we can see a convergence of the midcentury design influences incorporated by both Rand and Steinweiss.

From the shared aesthetic that Rand and Steinweiss created in their unique areas of visual design, their lifetimes of work still have a significant influence on the way brand identity programs are created and the way contemporary management views the critical contributions made by designers.

As Steven Heller said in summing up Steinweiss's career, "Steinweiss had launched a brand new field . . . his album covers defined music for a generation, maybe more. Today Steinweiss's record covers—really miniposters that continue to draw the eye—must be judged for how

---

Opposite top left and right: An early Steinweiss album cover from 1942 and an early 1943 advertisement by Rand

Opposite bottom left and right: Two album covers created by Steinweiss in the 1950s

ONCERTO IN F

LEVANT

KOSTELANETZ

LHARMONIC-SYMPHONY ORCHESTRA OF NEW YORK

COLUMBIA MASTERWORKS

the Walky-Talky by Emerson that dropped 5000 feet . . .

The earth comes up with a rush. The landing isn't easy. But that doesn't stop the tough little Walky-Talky by Emerson, that rode down beside the paratrooper on his rush through the hostile air.

Built to withstand shock and abuse . . . to come through slashing, swirling sand-storm and numbing cold . . . that's the Walky-Talky by Emerson. Forecast of the future . . . of the Emerson-built equipment you will enjoy in peace-time.

Not the least will be a compact, tough, little receiving set . . . your companion . . . whether fishing, sailing or skiing . . . an instrument that will need no more care or attention than your camp frying pan.

Yes, and other marvels learned in the grim business of War are taking shape today in the Emerson Electronic Laboratories . . . products of the *world's largest maker of home radio sets.*

EMERSON RADIO & PHONOGRAPH CORPORATION, NEW YORK 11, N. Y.
Buy extra war bonds and stamps today!

Emerson ELECTRONIC RADIO

EVEREST

oody oody

Woody Herman and his orchestra with Charlie Byrd, guitar

featuring "Summer Sequence"

they revolutionized music packaging, as well as how they influenced styles and fashions during the music industry's adolescence."

Steinweiss retired to Florida in 1973, creating 2,500 album covers over a thirty-four-year career. Long after his retirement, his modest nature and his unique talent are both evident as he reflected on an appearance at the AIGA.

> In 1989 I was invited by the AIGA to present a slide lecture on my career as a graphic designer. I was invited to sit down with 25 young graphic artists for a "meet the designer" session. I was seventy-two years old, and had long since retired from the graphic design business. . . . I was flattered that the AIGA extended the invitation . . . the average age was about 30 . . . despite the differences in working methods, there was a positive reaction to my work and a general feeling of amazement that it was done "by hand."

Steinweiss died in 2011 at the age of ninety-four, after living quietly with his wife, Blanche, in Sarasota, Florida. They met on Brighton Beach in Brooklyn in 1932 and had been married seventy-one years.

These two designers each had similar backgrounds, interests, and influence, yet practiced in very different corners of the brand design

Above: Early print media created by Paul Rand

Opposite: Corporate identity program created by Paul Rand

field. Steinweiss had an audience of primarily musicians and audio-
philes while Rand's work was meant for the corporate board room.

As Steven Heller also suggests,

> *Rand was a pioneering functionalist who relied on strong visual ideas
> and dynamic typography to convey a message. In the 1930s when
> American commercial art and advertising was dominated by hardsell
> copy and realistic illustration, Paul Rand introduced the formal
> vocabulary of the 1920s European avant-garde art movements. He was
> one of only a few American designers to lay claim to the Modernist
> traditions of Cubism, De Stijl, Constructivism and the Bauhaus, and
> was influential in bringing "The New Typography"—the rejection of
> archaic and sentimental type and layout treatments—to the United
> States. In later years, Rand continued to be a staunch proponent of
> Modern design as both a practitioner and author.*

Paul Rand passed on November 26, 1996, at the age eighty-nine. Even
in death, he was the ultimate designer with his headstone designed by
Swiss designer and colleague Fred Troller. Standing out from the more
traditional memorials, the pair of stacked marble cubes are a perfect
example of his commitment to design and its function in building
timeless brand identities.

The Modern
Brand Landscape

17

THE "GREATEST GENERATION" OF BRANDS: MARLBORO, MINUTE RICE, AND MR. CLEAN

Postwar America experienced a unique period of explosive consumer market growth influenced by the intersection of three factors: the previous three decades of economic depression and world war created pent-up demand; a maturing market dominated by mass production, mass marketing, and mass consumption; and the development of a completely new approach to commercial and retail infrastructure.

In his book *The Greatest Generation*, television journalist Tom Brokaw traces the formative beginning of the people living in this moment:

> *They were born in a time of national promise, optimism, and prosperity, when all things seemed possible. . . . What those unsuspecting infants could not have realized, of course, was that these were temporary conditions. . . . By the time these young Americans . . . had reached the age of ten, their earlier prospects were shattered. In 1938 our young American reached the age of 18, and the flames of war were everywhere. . . . By 1940 it was clear to all but a few delusional isolationists that war would define this generation's coming of age.*

They were in their early twenties when World War II broke out. After the giddiness of the 1920s, the tumult of the 1930s, and the tragedy of the early 1940s, they turned thirty in the 1950s. Millions of them came home to a world radically altered by the previous three decades, dreaming of finally settling down. Buying a house was central to the dream of raising their families—thus starting the baby boom generation.

Elaine Tyler May in her book *Homeward Bound* recounts the Kitchen Debate between Vice President Richard Nixon and the Soviet Premier Nikita Khrushchev, which took place at a commercial fair in Moscow in 1959: "It is important to keep in mind that the ideal home that Nixon described was one that both obliterated class distinctions and accentuated gender distinctions. The model home he extolled was not a mansion but the modest ranch-style structure."

William Levitt, developer of three Levittown communities and considered by many to have had a major influence on the growth of suburbia in the post-World War II era, said of home ownership, "No man who owns his own house and lot can be a Communist. He has too much to do."

Above: The 1950s was a time to settle down, buy a house, and start a family according to Nixon at the Kitchen Debate in Moscow.

Opposite: The TV became a selling machine in many living rooms.

Demographics of the time certainly paralleled the growth of a consumer culture. Between 1947 and 1961, the number of families rose 28 percent. National income increased 50 percent between 1935 and 1950, then 60 percent more during the 1950s. And the number of Americans with discretionary income doubled.

In the five years after World War II, consumer spending rose 60 percent, but spending for household furnishings and appliances rose 240 percent, spending on clothing rose only 20 percent, and spending on food rose 33 percent.

It soon became less expensive to own a new home than to rent. Financing was largely supplied through the new postwar Federal Housing Administration and Veteran's Administration loan programs. Home purchases went from just 114,000 in 1944 to a record 1,692,000 in 1950. In 1946, for the first time, the majority of Americans lived in a home that they owned.

As May points out, from 1946 to 1950, Americans purchased 21.4 million cars, 20 million refrigerators, 5.5 million stoves, 11.6 million TVs, and 1 million new homes per year.

In 1950, only 10 percent of households had a TV; just five years later, that figure was 67 percent, and by the end of the decade, it was 87 percent.

May continues,

> The impact of suburbia on consumer behavior can hardly be
> overstated . . . young people chose to marry early, have several children
> in early years of marriage, live in nice neighborhoods, and have cars,
> washing machines, refrigerators, television sets. Purchasing a home
> helped alleviate traditional American uneasiness with consumption . . .
> a fear that spending would lead to decadence. This new consumerism
> was a reinforcement of the Puritan ideal of pragmatism and morality,
> rather than opulence and luxury. Spending money on everything that
> went into a home was OK, and culturally acceptable.

Spending for the family reassured consumers and strengthened the
new American way of life. As May suggests, the goods purchased were
intended to foster traditional values. Homes were designed for enjoy-
ment, fun, and togetherness. Family members would not need to go out
for recreation since they had swing sets, playrooms, and backyards
with barbecues.

And of course a TV was in the middle of most living rooms. Television
delivered a consistent cultural message, and it brought brands directly
into the home. Advertising expenditures tripled between 1945 and 1959.
An NBC instructional film called the TV "a selling machine in every
living room."

The following three brands exemplify the new trends in consumption
driven by the dynamics of the postwar world. Each was aimed directly at
the generation that had survived the war and was enthusiastically and
dramatically increasing its personal consumption. These brands represent three trends: the evolution of postwar gender roles, the growth of
products for the home, and the increasing interest in convenience.

Marlboro

Uniquely, Marlboro was one of the few filter cigarettes initially positioned specifically for women. It even had a red band printed on the tip
to reduce residual lipstick stains.

In 1954, with new cancer questions beginning to surface, Philip Morris
repositioned the brand, with the help of the Leo Burnett ad agency, as
a filter cigarette for men. It would have a new filter, more flavor in a
new tobacco blend, and a crushproof flip-top box. The carton's structure was designed by the Molins Machine Company of Germany, and

Opposite: Marlboro's target consumer moved from women to men
in the 1950s.

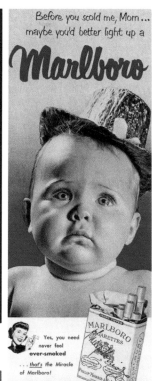

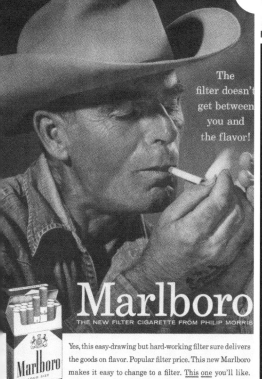

REVOLUTIONARY NEW RIC

NO OTHER RICE LIKE IT!

Just add to boiling water
to make
PERFECT RICE
instantly!

MINUTE
BRAND
RICE PERFECT EVERY TIME

PRE-COOKED

No washing! No rinsing!
No draining! No steaming!

the package graphics were by Frank Gianninoto Associates in New York. As the Leo Burnett agency said, "the new Marlboro smoker is a lean relaxed outdoorsman—a cattle rancher, a Navy officer, a flyer— whose tattooed wrist suggested a romantic past, a man who had once worked with his hands, who knew the score, who merited respect."

By the end of the 1950s, the Marlboro man had become the iconic and universally recognized cowboy that has been used to represent the brand for over sixty years.

Mr. Clean

Launched with a national television campaign in 1958, Mr. Clean became the best-selling household cleaner on the market within six months and for over sixty-five years has remained a unique brand supported by its recognizable icon.

Minute Rice

Minute Rice reflected a new age in food preparation and the suburban lifestyle of simplification and convenience. Introduced in 1949 by General Foods, it was the first instant rice that could cook in just a few minutes.

Above left: Mr. Clean is still a prominent brand icon more than sixty-five years after his introduction.

Above right: Minute Rice was introduced as a brand that could simplify everyday food preparation.

18

THE EXPLOSION OF SUBURBAN SHOPPING AND THE MALL

Immediately after World War II, the vast majority of population growth in the US happened in the suburbs. This growth obviously had an influence on the physical nature of the towns where it occurred, but just as importantly, it had a permanent impact on the commerce and cultural futures of those towns.

Elaine Tyler May describes this growth in Lawrence B. Glickman's book *Consumer Society in American History*:

> *Between 1950 and 1970 the suburban population in the U.S. doubled, from 36 million to 74 million . . . 83% of the nation's growth during those years took place in the suburbs. By stimulating these particular kinds of suburban housing developments and providing subsidies to homeowners, the federal government effectively underwrote the baby boom, along with the lifestyle and community arrangements.*

By the mid-1950s, the new suburban environment was reshaping the community marketplace. In *Consumer's Republic*, Lizabeth Cohen quotes the political scientist Robert Wood, who said that "by the 1950s the shopping center . . . had become as much a part of suburbia as the rows of houses, split-levels, and Cape Cods. Consumer spending reshaped much more than the character of residential communities in the post war metropolitan landscape. The physical arrangement of American commercial life became reconfigured as well."

One measure of this growth is the suburban share of total metropolitan retail trade in the ten largest metropolitan centers. It was 4 percent in 1939, 31 percent in 1948, and 61 percent in 1961.

This consumption took place in the new suburban shopping centers, a venue almost unknown before World War II and not planned into most communities by developers and homebuilders. Three early shopping centers included Kansas City's Country Club Plaza, Fair Lawn's Radburn (New Jersey), and Houston's River Oaks Center.

The first were simple "strip" centers along the new highways. Gradually groups of retailers built regional shopping centers—a new kind of environment offering a more modern and convenient combination of the retail, commercial, and civic duties of a traditional downtown.

Cohen talks about three new issues inherent in these evolving retail environments. Each had major effects on the marketplaces of the post-war era, including the commercializing, privatizing, and feminizing of public space.

Commercializing Public Space

Until the middle of the twentieth century, the marketplace was a public space where people of all kinds congregated, with a mix of commercial and civic agendas. That changed dramatically in the 1950s.

Shopping center planners believed they were contributing to a new way of life in ways that were just as important as how the new network of interstate highways transformed transportation and real estate developers delivered mass single-family housing.

Victor Gruen, designer of the Southdale Center in Edina, Minnesota, the first modern enclosed shopping mall, called them "shopping towns" and "crystallization points for suburbia's community life." His ideal was to recreate the civic activity and vibrance of a central public market, without its inconveniences.

Shopping centers addressed complaints about traditional downtown environments for new suburban families. Parking was plentiful, private security guards conveyed safety, truck traffic was kept away from the shoppers, covered walks and air conditioning made shopping comfortable all year, and the chains and franchise stores within sold predictable and fashionable merchandise.

Paramus, New Jersey, built two major shopping centers in the early 1950s that had a dramatic impact on the city. Retail sales nearly doubled in ten years, from $400 million USD in 1948 to $700 million USD in 1954, and almost 25 percent more to $866 million USD by 1958.

Built over fifty years ago, the Paramus Park Mall, Westfield Garden State Plaza, the Outlets at Bergen Town Center, and the Fashion Center still account for a major portion of retail sales in the county. Today, Paramus generates over $6 billion USD in annual retail sales—more than any other zip code in the US in spite of the stores being closed on Sundays.

In a classic pattern repeated throughout the US, the large urban city centers of New York and Newark saw a significant drop in their percentage of shoppers. Department stores saw their sales from

Opposite: A classic 1950s development in Levittown, Pennsylvania

suburban stores go from 4 percent of sales in 1951 to 32 percent in 1959, then to over half of total sales by 1966. Specialty retail stores had a similar increase from 6 percent to 33 percent in the same period. Lizabeth Cohen wrote, "As retail dollars moved out of major cities and away from established downtowns within suburban areas, regional shopping centers became the distinctive public space of the postwar landscape."

Privatizing Public Space

With the commercialization of public space, came the struggle to define political behavior permissible in the new, privately owned public spaces of the shopping centers. Cohen notes, "When the Red Cross organized blood drives, when labor unions picketed stores in organizing campaigns, when political candidates ran for office . . . they all viewed the shopping center as the obvious place to reach masses of people."

But these privately owned centers were wary of anything that made shoppers feel uncomfortable, and in a series of Supreme Court cases, it became clear that only speech of certain kinds was lawful. For instance, when ruling on a labor dispute (*Hudgens v. NLRB*) the court held that the First Amendment did not guarantee the right to this kind of free speech in privately owned shopping centers. Courts have also ruled that the right to demonstrate in support of consumer boycotts is not unlimited.

Feminizing Public Space

Lastly, Cohen points out that for centuries women had been the primary shoppers for the family and that many commercial spaces had been designed to appeal to the female shopper. But the traditional street environment, with a retail and business mix was not planned specifically for a female consumer.

These new shopping centers, conceived from the very start to be a comforting space where a woman could shop with a family, created the equivalent of a downtown district dedicated primarily to female consumption. Jack Follet, the president of John Graham and Company, an architectural firm that designed over seventy shopping malls, said of this trend, "I wouldn't know how to design a shopping center for a man."

Yes, the 1950s was a period of explosive growth, but as the decade ended, marketers realized that demand would not continue to grow at the unprecedented postwar pace. The days when Mr. Clean could become the best-selling household cleaner in months with simply TV advertising were over.

As demand ebbed in the recession of 1957 marketing shifts were emerging . Planned product upgrades became a marketing tool perfected by industries like auto, fashion, and technology.

Above: A scene of an early shopping center

Additionally, as new cultural divisions began to emerge, market segmentation was increasingly considered for ad campaigns.

As Lizabeth Cohen says,

> *In sum, by the late 1960s and early 1970s the conjunction of marketers seeking alternatives to mass marketing and consumers asserting their independence from what they perceived to be mainstream American culture bred an explosion in market segmentation. What resulted was a new commercial culture that reified—at times even exaggerated—social difference in the pursuit of profits, often reincorporating disaffected groups into the commercial marketplace.*

19

A REVOLUTIONARY DECADE FOR BRANDS

Without question, the 1960s were a tumultuous time. As James Baldwin—African American novelist, playwright, civil and gay rights activist, and one of the most heralded observers of the twentieth century—noted while writing about Rev. Martin Luther King Jr. and the civil rights struggles of the 1960s, "We will need every ounce of moral stamina we can find. For everything is changing, from our notion of politics to our notion of ourselves, and we are certain as we begin history's strangest metamorphosis . . . to undergo the torment of being forced to surrender far more than we ever realized we had accepted."

Brands underwent a similar transformation. The decade's cultural and commercial lessons, and its conflicting emotions, unfolded across five critical issues where brands would struggle.

The Growing Sophistication of Mass Communication

The 1960s began with an evolving combination of media and advertising, demonstrated by its use in selling brands as diverse as presidential candidates, government action, popular music, and the Volkswagen Beetle. In some ways, advertising became the revolution. As Hazel Warlaumont, former professor of communications at California State University, said in her book *Advertising in the 60s*, "Advertising and the 1960s were an odd alliance. . . . Targeted by the counterculture, threatened with government regulation, criticized as a 'waste maker' by social critics, weakened by internal conflict, and faced with a consumption-weary public, advertising faced one of its most challenging times."

In 1960, Doyle Dane Bernbach (DDB) introduced its iconic Volkswagen campaign. With this initiative, DDB was leading a shift in advertising from copy-heavy to image-driven communication, where the product presentation was often the hero. The modernist photography on white seamless backgrounds was supported by insightful copy that featured a simple headline, with both containing a strong sense of irony.

Founded in 1949, the agency pioneered an intelligent approach to selling, reflected in some of its earlier work for Levy's Rye and Avis. When speaking of advertising, agency founder Bill Bernbach was noted as saying, "All of us who professionally use the mass media are the shapers of society. We can vulgarize that society. We can brutalize it. Or we can help lift it onto a higher level."

It should be noted that all great agencies have a deep and critical talent pool. At DDB, it included the art director Helmut Krone, widely considered one of the most significant leaders of modern advertising, and the pioneering copywriter Bob Levenson.

Reflecting a relentless search for truth in advertising, Bob Levenson entered a 1960 Time Inc. ad industry contest that invited agencies to create an advertisement in the public interest. His iconic advertisement titled "Do This or Die." was the result. This was an ad with no visual

Above: Early VW ad and *Time* magazine's public-interest advertisement written by Bob Levenson

Opposite: An Avis promotional button

imagery other than that conjured by intensely frank and critical language. He took direct aim at what he viewed as the deceptive, untruthful, and infantile content in much of the advertising at the time. His key point, communicated with incredibly direct copy, was that the industry should strive to use its talent and skill in a search for truth.

In 1963, also with the help of DDB, Krone, and copywriter Paula Green, Avis began its "We Try Harder" advertising campaign by promoting being the number 2 rental agency—another example of an approach that rejected the naiveté of competing brands with growing sophistication and ironic copy.

In the mid-1960s, Wells Rich Green was founded, and Mary Wells Lawrence became the first woman to lead an advertising agency. She came out of Doyle Dane Bernbach and was a leading figure in workplace advances for women in marketing and branding.

She also clearly expressed exasperation with her early experiences in advertising during the 1950s and did everything she could to fight the trends of creating cynical content as pointed out by Bob Levenson's "Do This or Die" ad. Her campaign for Braniff Airlines represents another example of the growing sophistication in mass communication in two ways—the use of clever, ironic copy and graphics from an iconic modern artist. Specifically, the ad leads with the headline containing a double entendre "Introducing the Air Strip," and the campaign's design system incorporates delightful and engaging airplane graphics rendered by the artist Alexander Calder—a logical extension of Steinweiss's and Rand's adoption of modern art in their work.

As Lawrence noted in her book *A Big Life (in Advertising)*,

> *America hungered for happiness and peace, so they produced advertising that was happy and peaceful. Children were always clean and smiling. Dogs were clean and smiling. Firemen, police, farmers, and coal miners were clean and smiling. Everybody waved to each other in the ads. Beautiful women stretched out on the roofs of cars . . . to make the cars look prettier. Bottles of whiskey had crowns and stood proudly on red velvet columns. Bill [Bernbach] was right; advertising was a land of the insane.*

In spite of these expressed concerns by Wells and others, the postwar consumer market continued to grow in sophistication, empathy, and diversity. While exploring a number of ways to respond to the new cultural trends of the era, brands continued to identify ways of speaking to an increasingly complex marketplace.

As the industry's lead publication *Ad Age* has said about the period, "The 1960s were advertising's 'coming of age,' when the industry mastered the language of TV, appropriated the medium of photography,

Above: Mary Wells Lawrence's Braniff Airlines advertising with airplane graphics by Alexander Calder

and produced work of unprecedented creativity. Influenced by the cultural and social changes of the decade, advertising reflected a trend toward innovation, sophistication and a growing youth culture."

The Loss of Innocence

During the 1960s—with the growing dissatisfaction with the Vietnam War, student protests around the globe, and assassinations of prominent figures—almost half the population was under the age of twenty-five, making the country younger than at any time in its history. Brands, addressing the baby boom generation for the first time, needed to find ways to confront this new consumer force. As Warlaumont said about the generation during this decade, "its artifacts, the cultural revolution, the legendary music, bizarre fashions, radical politics, innovative art, and hip rhetoric, remain etched in time, to resurface frequently it seems, and be questioned endlessly."

In 1966, the Psychedelic Shop opened in the Haight-Ashbury neighborhood of San Francisco. It was a physical reflection of this cultural phenomenon of liberation and revolution—cultural historian David McNally called the Psychedelic Shop "the linchpin to the world's first psychedelic neighborhood."

By 1967, the psychedelic poster movement had begun in San Francisco for bands like Grateful Dead and in London for groups like Pink Floyd, and *Life* magazine published a cover story on this poster art. The movement's most obvious contemporary influences and subject matter were the hallucinogenic images of the drug culture. These posters also took inspiration from earlier artistic styles of art nouveau and expressionism, often using the dreamlike quality of surrealism and the strong colors of fauvism.

Many poster artists were self-taught, but not all. Victor Moscoso was classically trained, having studied at San Francisco Art Institute and later at Cooper Union and at Yale with Joseph Albers, one of the foremost modern artists and art teachers of the twentieth century.

The Woodstock Music and Art Fair of 1969 brought the decade to an end. With an attendance of nearly five hundred thousand young people, it represented a cultural turning point for the music business. Importantly, it became a defining moment in the counterculture movement and has since often been referenced by brands that reflect the interests of this generation and its admirers.

The Limitations of Commercial Creativity

During the 1960s, as large corporate brands began to demonstrate a unified approach to their identities, a sameness became the visual expression of modern society.

One approach often labeled "midcentury design" came to prominence. This was a period when corporate branding went international, and abstract and symbolic work began to have a strong influence. The work of Paul Rand, Lester Beall, and Chermayeff and Geismar led the way. Its beginnings were with the simplicity of the Bauhaus and the intellectual discipline of the study of signs and symbols that convey meaning. In the early years of the decade, corporate programs for Chase Manhattan, International Paper, Westinghouse, and UPS were typical of this genre.

As various art movements began to shine a new light on the role of consumer brands in society and the images that reflect it, Andy Warhol had his first solo exhibition of pop art at the Ferus Gallery in Los Angeles in 1962.

Warhol is famously quoted as saying, "Commercial art is real art and real art is commercial art." His work was a consistent reminder of the overlapping nature of brands, commerce, aesthetics, design, and art. Trained as a commercial artist and illustrator, he was one of the first American artists to highlight the dual role of the objects and methods of mass commerce by having both commercial and cultural value.

The celebrities of the time were not the traditional royalty and church elders but movie stars, and the simple visual pleasures of food still life paintings had begun to morph into images of the prepared-food world we now take for granted.

Opposite top left: An example of the youth counterculture of the 1960s—a poster for Woodstock music festival

Opposite top right: Andy Warhol and a can of Campbell's Soup, which became a central image of the Pop Art movement

Opposite bottom: The work of the Vignellis

The graphic and product design work created by Massimo and Lella Vignelli is another example of the multiple visual influences that created a unique simplicity and craft for the brands they touched. Their work was as diverse as the new Knoll logo and brand-identity program to housewares that are still best-sellers for Heller. However, their iconic New York subway graphics, while visually striking, were an overly simplistic abstraction with little connection to the underlying geographic references, later rejected for something less abstract.

Consumer Protection

It can be argued that the third wave of consumer activism began in 1962 with the presentation of a Consumer Bill of Rights and President John F. Kennedy declaring, "Consumers, by definition, include us all . . . they are the only important group . . . who are not effectively organized, whose views are often not heard. The consumer is the only man in our economy without a high-powered lobbyist. I intend to be that lobbyist."

Above: Two examples of 1960s consumer activism, including Ralph Nader's 1965 book *Unsafe at Any Speed* and the appearance of smoking warnings on cigarette packages

Opposite: Two examples of human rights photography: Jack Thornell's image of an injured James Meredith just after he had been shot and Joseph Ambrosini's image of the first night of the Stonewall Riots

Importantly, this set of principles encompassed four fundamental rights, including the right to be informed, the right to safety, the right to choose, and the right to be heard.

The Divisiveness of Racism, Sexism, and Gay Rights

The symbols and icons of the civil, gay, and women's rights movements of the 1960s first appeared in news media and featured people like Muhammad Ali, Jack and Bobby Kennedy, Rosa Parks, Lyndon Johnson, Betty Friedan, and John Lewis.

These images were not carefully conceived and rendered design solutions. Their strength comes from their immediacy and their depiction of a significant moment. And unlike the artists and designers previously mentioned, the creators of this legacy were photojournalists.

Images of student sit-ins that began in North Carolina, James Meredith being admitted to the University of Mississippi, Martin Luther King Jr. giving the "I Have a Dream" speech, the assassination of Malcom X, and Friedan, founder of the National Organization of Women, author of *The Feminine Mystique*, lobbying the New York State Assembly, each preserve the spirit of the decade for posterity.

Importantly, to the extent that these social movements have become brands, more than sixty years later, they continue to live through these images.

They were taken by people like Jack Thornell of the Associated Press, who took the Pulitzer Prize-winning photo of James Meredith just after he had been shot at the Mississippi March Against Fear, or the freelance photographer Joseph Ambrosini, who took the only known photograph during the first night of New York's Stonewall Riots.

During the 1960s, marketers came to view their audience as a diverse collection of ever-changing lifestyles and interests. Never again would consumers be viewed as a monolithic group. During this decade, society began its journey toward the extraordinarily diverse media environment that the twenty-first century now presents.

20

THE CURRENT EVOLUTION OF RETAIL IN FOUR STEPS

In 1900, 13 percent of the world's population lived in cities. By 2050, the number will rise to at least 70 percent. In 1950, there were two cities with metropolitan populations of 10 million. Today there are at least thirty-four, and that number is growing quickly.

For brand marketers, the evolution of this growth and how to accommodate it has had a direct influence on the direction and structure of the retail experience. Retail has evolved into four very different types of venues, leading to four very different experiences. Each represents a critical link in the evolution of consumer experience, and each has a direct impact on brands and retail package design.

It should be stressed that while these four marketplace constructs evolved during very different times and for very different reasons, each is still a vital and vibrant part of modern retailing.

Retail 1.0—Commodities Become Goods

This is the oldest retail form and has existed since at least 3000 BCE. The conversation in this marketplace has been directly between the merchant/craftsperson and the shopper, and this conversation has always been human to human.

Opposite left: An example of Retail 1.0—open-air market in Novgorod, Russia

Opposite right: An example of Retail 2.0—a small grocery store in Chicago, Illinois

The nature of this transaction has always been very personal and remains so today. It is best represented by the ancient global bazaars, souks, agoras, and marketplaces, which, of course, are still a vibrant part of today's retail environment.

For the last several millennia, the transaction involved no brands, merely commodities that were promoted and sold only with the trust in the merchant, such as a farmer, baker, or butcher.

Retail 2.0—Goods Become Brands

This form existed before the mid-eighteenth-century beginnings of the industrial revolution. The conversations were between business and consumer. They were very unequal, with proprietors, shopkeepers, and staff mediating as a brand and product filter.

As consumers participated in an increasingly branded mass market, their relationships with large consumer product companies became mutually dependent.

Retail 2.0 is best represented by a new and growing variety of retail, including independent urban shops and chain grocery stores like A&P. These locations carried a larger number of brands, both private label and national—each selected carefully by the merchant. As a result, many of the purchase decisions were influenced by the shop owner-ship and sales staff.

The final evolution of Retail 2.0 took place during the twenty years on either side of the turn of the twentieth century. Shopping became a

major part of household work, and shoppers were now consumers of the mass-market economy.

Retail 3.0—Brands Become Experiences

Retail 3.0, and the era of the self-service market, began with the opening of the first Piggly Wiggly grocery store in Memphis in 1916. Radically, it was self-service, where consumers could freely select brand and product choices on their own, uninfluenced by and liberated from the salesclerks. Direct conversations began between brands and shoppers at the point of sale.

This was a truly revolutionary concept for its time and was laid out in aisles where customers could see, touch, and read the packages of all the merchandise. The package was now the primary brand communicator and motivator. The freedom to make one's own choices at the point of sale led quickly to a new emphasis on branded products, with brand identities and package designs supported by new forms of print and broadcast media. This collectively redefined the relationships between manufacturers, wholesalers, retailers, and consumers. And for a century, the Retail 3.0 model represented most of the growth in global retail.

Above: An example of Retail 3.0—a contemporary Walmart

Opposite: An example of Retail 4.0—an online virtual department store

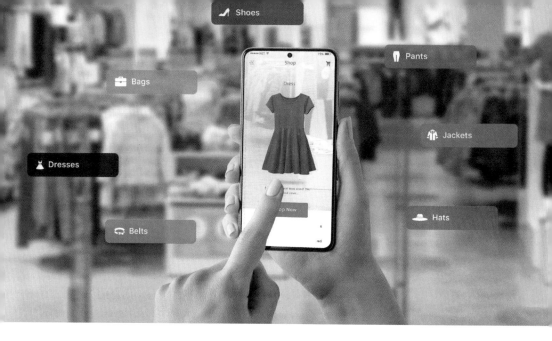

Retail 4.0—Brand Experiences Become Communities

Beginning in the twenty-first century, Retail 4.0 is best seen as a conversation shared between consumers, retailers, and brands. Consumers, influencers, retailers, manufacturers, and brand owners—both in store and out—all speak, listen, and have almost constant exchanges that directly influence patterns of consumption. These conversations, as omni-channel experiences, are not limited to any one physical store format, and the package is no longer the only, or in some instances, the main, brand communicator.

Like with Gutenberg in the fifteenth century, we live in a time when access to information is being transformed by technology. As a result, we live in a global retail marketplace with omnipresent brand messages. Thanks to current communications technology, purchase decisions are often live-shared, with purchasers engaging with their self-defined communities.

As David Kepron says in *Retail (r)Evolution*, "The connections brands make with their customers are cemented through fostering empathetic relationships with experiences rich in storytelling, ritual and play."

Today's Brand

21

THE TWENTY-FIRST-CENTURY HUNTER-GATHERER CULTURE AND HOW WE SEARCH

With the ubiquity of Retail 4.0, we are in the early stages of the most dramatic change in retail branding and package design in over a century. But brands can meet the challenges of an omni-channel lifestyle across blended retail/e-tail environments if they understand the four search patterns that consumers use to locate, assess, and select.

Successful search techniques have always been pivotal to the survival of our species, from the ancient skill of divining water to our ability to locate the newest hard seltzer. Innovation, invention, and evolving tools and technologies have refined human search patterns for tens of thousands of years.

Search Methodology Number One: "Let's Go Back"

Imagine you have been camped along a riverbank all winter—you're thirsty—and you know that the river has predictably supplied you with fresh clean water under the ice. Almost without thinking, and certainly without any hesitation, you go down to the river and drink.

This search pattern is predictable, safe, and comfortable, and the outcome is reliable, without stress. It is similar to buying everyday products like milk, paper towels, and toothpaste. In these categories, most of the time, we are on autopilot as we fill our baskets.

These categories are characterized by a high level of trust and brand loyalty, like the baby diaper category, where 85 percent of purchasers typically select between one or two brands.

The visual characteristics of these brands are incredibly predictable, as they should be when searching for the safety of familiar products. Many brands share overwhelmingly universal imagery. For instance, in the baby diaper category, the visual equity of all major brands includes the following:

- Soft, pudgy, baby-like typography for the brand logo that supports the warm, cuddly nature of product usage.

- One bright main color for each brand—key in a category where most design architectures are similar and brand differentiation is necessary.

- Package architecture that contains soft, gentle shapes—again, this is predictable given the product category's brand experience.

- Baby photography, because who doesn't love the image of a cute baby? This key visual element makes the brand image safe, comfortable, and expected.

Above: An example of a shopping aisle in a familiar search category

Brands that rely on familiarity must sustain the historical "let's go back" impulse in a blended retail environment. They can do so by using all the brand's intrinsic visual tools of familiarity, warmth, and ease of connection. The brand must look like it belongs to the product category yet is unique enough to capture interest. The familiar-search brand thrives on intentional uniformity and should enhance and encourage a comfortable consumer connection.

Search Methodology Number Two: "That Reminds Me"

Imagine you are traveling down a path on a new and unfamiliar mountainside—you are hungry—and as you crest a hillside, you look down and see fields filled with familiar bushes. As you approach them, you recognize the berries and spend the afternoon devouring them with pleasure. Your willingness to try the berries you know in a place you've never been is a search informed by learned experience. While something about the circumstance may be new, your experience suggests it will be good for you.

If our story took place in a supermarket aisle, why might a consumer reach for your brand? It could be a visual element like a logo or the package's shape. When searching in a field of berries, or a retail environment, we gravitate toward things we have associations with. It is a measure of comfort that comes from a brand you trust. While you may not have bought this brand's breakfast cereal, you have had good experiences with its other products. You are intrigued and confident because, as with the berries, it reminds you of a pleasant experience.

A consumer's recognition, experience, and trust are part of brand equity. Visually, a package, a logo, and other design elements wrap brand equity into a physical object. For example, the power of a brand's color and logo can grab a consumer's attention and create immediate recognition.

The brand marketer's challenge is deciding how to use their brand's equity across a diverse product family. And when introducing a brand with new products or in new categories, they must ask if the brand is essential to product messaging or whether it's better to minimize the brand presence.

By understanding consumers' associations with a brand and what brand equity exists and what signals or cues a shopper would look for or notice, we aim for immediate recognition in a refreshed or new product line extension pack.

Above: A Seagram's Gin line extension product that takes advantage of consistent and well-recognized brand image elements

Opposite: The innovative new product packaging launched for Vermont Spirits Vintage Vodka

Search Methodology Number Three: "Let's Explore"

Imagine paddling down a river and coming to a familiar bend, where you have always taken the right fork. But today, you are feeling adventurous, so you go left instead. Soon you come upon the shore of a small sandbar, where low tide has exposed oyster beds that you and your family feast on for several days. This story of curiosity and adventure is an analogy for a consumer search pattern called free search—where creating brands that rely on experimentation and curiosity is critical.

When shoppers are in the mood to explore, they are looking for the unexpected, the new, the intriguing. In each product category, those visual motivators may be different, but the emotions are the same.

Pictured is an example of a product optimized for the free-search methodology—a new super-premium vodka. Vermont Spirits Vintage is a hand-crafted, super-premium vodka distilled only once a year, in the heart of the Vermont countryside, using the purest first-run maple sap and spring water from the Green Mountains surrounding Quechee, Vermont.

The designer's task was to reflect this unique product's qualities: a result of the skill inherent in generations of New England sugarhouse and distilling traditions.

The alcoholic beverage category is well suited for free-search because consumers in this category are more than open to experimentation and exploration, and there are three trends that this brand design has responded to. There is a rising interest in more premium choices, a

Above: A detail page from the RoC Skincare website, which contains starred review rankings

quest for authenticity gained from location, authorship, or heritage, and the use of unexpected materials, finishes, and printing methods. The final design strongly cued its Vermont heritage, maple source, and hand-crafted authenticity.

For consumers, free search is about curiosity and discovering the unknown. It's about the happy accident, the surprise, and exploration. Free-search brands can be inventive, innovative, and creative in return. Free search is all about discovery—and the freedom to explore.

Search Methodology Number Four: "Can You Help Me?"

You are traveling on horseback across an unfamiliar prairie when you meet an old friend. She has deep experience and local knowledge, and you are looking for a safe place to camp with your family, so you ask if she can help you. Her directions lead you to the perfect campsite, well protected from the wind and sun.

This story could have taken place thousands of years ago or just yesterday, and it is an analogy for a consumer search pattern we call influenced search. And if you believe, as I do, that humanity is defined by shared communities and cultures with shared values, you will see that influenced search is perhaps both the oldest and the newest of the four search patterns.

The foundation of this search is trust-seeking and relying on recommendations to influence your decision. On social media, information, reviews, and recommendations can direct virtually every brand decision that a consumer makes. Influencers are bent on impacting and often profiting from your choices. The institutionalization of influence has become a major part of promotional brand planning.

Marketers have several opportunities in a world where media activities and influences increasingly impact consumers' decisions. First, with so many more communications platforms, consumer information can be directed to a wide range of audiences and picked up and shared among media. Second, consumers appear to have an infinite number of choices, and they will search for the product that meets their needs best, strengthening the requirement for informed advice. Ultimately, influenced search will play a strategically important role in brand communication as the world becomes increasingly dominated by communities with shared brand and media interests. Recommendations are invaluable when consumers' searches are led by multiple layers of influence.

22

THE SEVEN VIRTUES AND RETAIL BRAND EXPERIENCE

This brings us to final thoughts based on the historical lessons of retailing and brand development introduced throughout this book. They are driven by my optimistic view that the technological tools leading commerce today will continue to be influenced by a core group of ancient, universal, and very human truths.

In a world filled with contemporary acronyms like AI, VR, QR, NFC, IOT, Wi-Fi, and RFID—each playing a critical role in an evolving marketplace—this discussion, like this book, will look back to go forward. It will draw from a group of seven traditional virtues first described by the sixth-century Pope Gregory and more recently elaborated in the thirteenth century by Saint Thomas Aquinas.

But first let me be clear: I do not pretend to be a theologian. Throughout my life, while having Quaker, Unitarian, and Congregational roots, I have not followed a traditional religious path. The path my faith has taken has been based on a humanistic devotion to intuition and creativity—two of humanity's truly unique capabilities—and their role in various areas of human endeavor.

Temperance

Temperance suggests a certain self-restraint and, in the case of marketing, the ability to be objective about your current successes, no matter how grand and seemingly invincible, and the acceptance that current success is no guarantee of future.

In 2017, for the first time ever, Americans spent more money in restaurants and bars than at grocery stores. This trend, in spite of Covid, has continued. In 2022, according to the US Census Bureau, Americans spent 20 percent more at restaurants than on groceries.

In 2024, the global rise in home delivery was led by one company with a series of notable attributes.

This company accepts orders from anywhere and at any time, and its supply chain dominates the competition. It utilizes cutting-edge distribution and delivery systems, carefully monitoring and recording every purchase. Detailed demographic information is kept on each of its billions of visitors. It has a loyalty program, which offers significant incentives. It sells both branded and private-label products and has begun adding retail stores to its primary business. All its competitors complain about an unfair advantage.

Yes, this describes Amazon. But back in 1897, this described Sears & Roebuck. While Sears was an overwhelming retailing giant in the nineteenth and twentieth centuries, dominating its competition, we all know what has happened to Sears in the twenty-first century. A bit more temperance by management might have saved this retail icon.

Wisdom

Speaking of Amazon, I think we can agree that it is a place filled with smart people, including its founder. During conversations with Amazon executives, I have learned two things. The first is that Jeff Bezos believes shopping is one of the most horribly inefficient ways of using time. So, smartly, Amazon spends a lot of time trying to make shopping more efficient, an experience that is rewarding and, just as importantly— though they may have a ways to go on this—I dare say fun.

And as the next step in Retail 4.0 evolves—or perhaps it will be a defining characteristic of a new Retail 5.0—it's possible that once autonomous vehicles are cheap, safe, and plentiful, these vehicles will be stores, and streets—not buildings—will be where commerce takes place. In fact, self-driving vehicles could make brick-and-mortar retail nearly obsolete in some local areas.

Courage

This virtue is not overlooked by smart marketers who speak about success and failure. In this context, the second thing I learned from Amazon is that it believes online shopping will soon represent 40 percent of the entire grocery market. A brave prediction indeed! While other sources believe we are in the beginning of this trend, most are nowhere near this estimate.

To get there, Amazon is looking to upend relationships between traditional retail brands and brick-and-mortar stores. For 150 years, these relationships have determined how all retail products are designed, promoted, packaged, and shipped.

If Amazon succeeds, brands will think less about how products are designed for and viewed on retail shelves. Instead, they will focus on designing products to accommodate a digital experience, ship quickly to customers' doorsteps, consider their end use, and have critical in-home advantages.

Marketers talk about the "moment of truth" as that magical retail instant when the relationship becomes a transaction. And since the nineteenth century, this has been package design's holy grail. Today, courageous marketers and retailers are envisioning the digital "moment of truth" to take brands forward.

Justice

This book has described the growth of brand communities and the conversations they encourage. In a world that is unbiased and just, commerce will be a shared and more equitable discussion, with consumers, brand owners, and retailers both speaking and listening. During the twentieth century, consumers increasingly were forced to enter into fundamentally unequal brand relationships that included themselves and very large global consumer product companies. When a new, more just discussion really begins to take hold, perhaps consumers will take back some of the control over brand decisions that they lost.

It will also be a DIY world where both the product and the package will become a medium that encourages interaction of both consumers and brand owners. With various kinds of digital printing technologies, we are entering a time when consumers, not just brand owners and the designers that serve them, can have a significant impact on the appearance of a brand in their home.

So, the question for all of us in these brand communities—including brand owners and designers—is how do we respond to a mutual discussion about brand creation responsibilities, where we must share a brand's visual equity creation in this new multifaceted environment?

To designers I would say, relax and worry!

Faith

Appropriately, Sheryl Sandberg, the former Facebook COO, writes the following about friendship in her foreword to Adam Grant's book *Originals*: "A friend is someone who sees more potential in you than you see in yourself, someone who helps you become the best version of yourself."

In this description of a friend, she could just as easily be describing our ideal relationship with and the faith we put in the brands we prefer. Those who build brands spend much of their time, energy, and intellectual capital on finding innovative ways of building consumer faith. In our increasingly digital world, the notion and value of friendship is constantly evolving and critically involves putting faith in these new relationships.

In our expanding social media environment, the influencer/friend relationships we have with brands are clearly evolving. But this evolution, while certainly secular, is really no different than the faith journey each of us—in our own way—have always traveled.

One final observation suggests that faith has always been connected to our vision of truth in the spiritual realm. Going forward, it may also be increasingly connected to one's secular vision of the brands we put faith in.

Hope

When we communicate with our friends, it's a conversation. We talk and listen in equal measures. Today in retail, we hear brand voices in a very one-sided conversation as we wander around Wegman's or Saks Fifth Avenue.

They are yelling "free offers," singing "free range," warning about "free radicals," whispering "sugar free." Asking to be taken home! Once home, they continue to yell, sing, warn, and whisper from behind our pantry walls and vanity doors.

I have a fervent hope that these moments will become more personalized and customized conversations, which suggests the following questions:

- **For marketers:** What should a brand's package say, and where, in this conversation?

- **For retailers:** How do I sell and display a package that also supports a digitally connected shopper?

- **For consumers:** What is the meaning and function of a brand's package in a cocurated world?

Love

Harvard Professor Gerald Zaltman's research suggests that 95 percent of our purchasing decisions are made subconsciously. Additionally, 75 percent of buying experiences are based on emotions.

So the most human of all virtues, the ability to love people, products, lifestyles, and experiences is inherent in who we are. Love drives our decision-making in virtually every aspect of our lives, including the brands we choose. And certainly, brand love has always been an elusive dream of all marketers.

Two retailer brands have done a good job bringing that message forward and shown us in the last few years that, with love, brands can bring us together.

The first is President's Choice, with its #EatTogether campaign. With this copy line, "What the world needs now is love sweet love ... Nothing brings us together like eating together!," they explored one impact of our digital culture.

The second is Walmart with its "Many Chairs. One Table" campaign, with the lyrics "If you hear the song I sing / You hold the key to love and fear / Everybody get together, try to love one another right now," which also explored another response to human connection.

As Richard Breitengraser, a global storyteller, content and marketing executive, and member of the Forbes Business Council has said,

> I'm advocating for a renaissance of the love-brand approach because, in times of blind focus on reach, conversion rates or endless expansion, I advise companies to take a serious look at their own brand, especially

Above: An image from the Walmart "Many Chairs. One Table" program

with a view toward customer lifetime value. But what makes love brands so special? They represent the highest level of connection between brands and customers. Unlike reach or awareness, you can't buy this status as a brand.

Simply put, the connection we have with our favorite brands is always, and will continue to be, a love story. With your help, and the help of the brand communities you hold most dear, we can keep it that way.

Acknowledgments

I am the son of two architects who, from birth, instilled in me a strong foundation in design. Importantly, they demonstrated that dedication to design, and each other, could be a couple's lifelong shared journey. For that I will be forever grateful.

My wife Pam and I met at our first job, both young designers in love with the exuberance of the 1970s Manhattan creative community and of course with each other. Since these early moments, we have been dedicated to our growing family—Alex, Scott, Tripp, Finn, Wyatt, and Millie—and sharing a design business we founded together over thirty years ago. This book, and so much else about my life, would not have been possible without Pam's support.

My career has been filled with moments of grace inspired by generous associates. This list begins with George Lois, Kurt Weihs, and Clive Chajet, who offered support in my first job. It continues with Walter Margulies, Irwin Susskind, Ron Peterson, Jack Blythe, and Bruce Macdonald. Today, at Invok Brands, I am inspired by a group of talented friends led by our partners Anne Marie Pagliacci and Michael Azulay.

Seventeen years ago, I became a founding faculty member of the Masters in Branding program at SVA. It would have been impossible without the support of my colleagues, teaching assistants, staff, and especially our hundreds of students.

In 2009, a master's degree in branding was unavailable anywhere in the world. The first step was to create an inspiring curriculum. To do this required serious research on my part and no one contributed more to that early effort than Grant McCracken, a friend and brilliant cultural anthropologist.

And then there is the incomparable Debbie. The SVA program would never have come together without the love and commitment of Debbie Millman. From the program's earliest hours, she has inspired us all us. Thank you, Debbie, for everything, every day for the last seventeen years.

Without Mark Kingsley this book would simply not exist. I needed convincing that this was necessary—he did it. Needed advice on how it could happen—he provided it. And needed unbiased comment on the content—he gave it.

About the Author

As an entrepreneur partner and chief creative officer of Invok Brands, **Richard Shear's** expertise lies in helping clients uncover the visual heritage of their most iconic brands and using this design equity to help them build and position these brands in ways that inform, connect, and motivate. As a member of the School of Visual Arts founding faculty of the Masters in Branding program, Richard teaches The History of Branding, focusing on the interconnected evolution of global consumer culture and visual history through the last two millennia and its influences on contemporary retail brands.

About the Series Editor

Mark Kingsley is a creative director and strategist with a wide range of experience and recognition. He is a faculty member in the School of Visual Arts Masters in Branding program and currently holds the endowed Melbert B. Cary Professorship in Graphic Arts at the Rochester Institute of Technology. As executive strategy director at Collins, he developed the new global positioning for Ogilvy and helped Equinox enter the luxury hotel business. For over seventeen years, his studio Greenberg Kingsley specialized in music and arts, including several years of branding and advertising for Central Park SummerStage; work for the Guggenheim Museum store; and music packaging for John Coltrane, Pat Metheny, and Quincy Jones. His current studio, Malcontent, serves global advertising firms, fin-tech startups, arts organizations, living legends, and Pulitzer Prize winners.

Index